HAVE A NICE DAY JOB

A humorous look at my career

as a park ranger, ecologist,

and park superintendent

David H. Van Cleve

A special thanks to Jeff Price, who collected and gave me permission to use many of the mixed metaphors, malaprops, and stupid statements used in these anecdotes.

To Mary

I would like to acknowledge all the "Parks People" who inspired me through their absolute devotion and dedication to the highest ideals of Parks work.

May, 2013

Cover: The author, feeding deer at Big Basin Redwoods State Park in the summer of 1956. A few years later, feeding deer was prohibited by park managers. The author worked at Rancho del Oso, part of Big Basin Redwoods SP, as a ranger in the mid-1970's. His duties included, well, you guessed it...

FROM WHENCE THE SPARK

I owe a lot of my success to my parents – especially my mother and father...

Boy, I must have really been destined to become a park ranger. I say this even though this was far from a lifelong dream. Au contraire, mon frère; I had not even considered this career option until late in my senior year in college. But then an amazing series of events occurred in a very short period of time that led to a great job that became a wonderfully satisfying career, pretty much as a surprise to me. A few months before graduating from college, I had not a clue about what job, much less a career, would be available to me. I had planned on being a teacher at an outdoor education camp, but when I did my practice teaching stint, it was clear that it was just not a good fit. Lack of discipline, lack of focus, screwing around in class and in the woods constantly – and the sixth-graders were even worse than I was! I needed to find a different path, and find it quickly.

As we consider the road that unfolds before us...

But before that, there was a life-changing occurrence that allowed these subsequent events to guide me. I had been at the

University of California at Santa Cruz for nearly two years, beginning in the fall of 1968. Let's just say that, um, life at Santa Cruz was different from my high school days. Of course, this was the 60's, and everything was changing rapidly and radically. I was going to be a literature major, or so I thought. UCSC was using the pass/fail system at the time (no grades) along with written evaluations by your professor. I passed my lit classes, but the dumb professors, in their evaluations of my work, kept saying things like, "David provides good plot summaries, but is lacking when it comes to rigorous analysis." I thought that when the old man went fishing in the sea, it was a story fit for the Outdoors section. What metaphor? What is a metaphor? I preferred mixed metaphors.

My mom said that when you sneeze, you should always cover your hand...

After almost two years at Santa Cruz, my parents were becoming frustrated with my progress there – they were all like "what progress?" and I was all like "progress...we don't need no stinkin' progress." Education is an end, not just a means, right? C'MON! In other words, I had not found a major, and there were few prospects in sight. Then I went to the first Earth Day ever, in the spring of 1970, held locally on the banks of the San Lorenzo River in Santa Cruz. There was a large number of booths and speakers, all urging environmental activism. It was very inspiring to me. To this day, when asked the question, "What sparked you to spend your adult life in the field of conservation?" I tell them it was that first Earth Day. Thank you, Senator Gaylord Nelson. I did not come from a family that had a history of camping and backpacking. This was all new to me, but it sure stuck.

At the same time, UCSC was creating a new major in Environmental Studies. So that fall I switched my major(s) to Geography and Environmental Studies, started taking really exciting classes, and was fortunate to have professors like Ray Collett and Ray Cooley. These guys were on the leading edge of environmental work. So my academic path became clear, but I still had no idea where this would lead vis-à-vis a job or career.

Skip ahead two years, to when I was a senior at UC Santa Cruz in early 1972, and fearful that my parents' prediction that my four years in college would be wasted was going to come true. One weekend in January, my roommate Bob and his girlfriend Suzy were invited to spend a Sunday afternoon as guests of Park Ranger Denzil Verardo and his wife Jenny at Big Basin Redwoods State Park. Suzy and Jenny had been friends at UCSC and had stayed in contact. The two women visited at the Verardos' park residence, while Denzil signed Bob up for a ride along through the park. Bob came home Sunday night as excited as I had ever seen him – certainly the most excited I had seen him since the night during our freshman year when sophomore Katy Kleinmeister decided to bestow her rather ample favors upon him. "We have got to become State Park Rangers!" was his new mantra. He described how Denzil got to live in the redwoods for very low rent and appeared to get paid for driving a truck around all day through a beautiful state park. It all sounded heavenly!

Bob and I hiked down to Henry Cowell Redwoods State Park (the park and the campus had evolved from the same ranch of Mr. Henry Cowell) later that week and asked the park staff how to get a job as a ranger. The clerk in the office said we had better hustle, because that very day was the final filing date for the State Park Ranger Trainee Civil Service Exam! We hustled off to the college placement center, filled out applications, and made sure they were postmarked that day. I was a little surprised that Bob was interested, since he was a Psychology major with a real talent in graphic design; he must have been surprised too, for he soon dropped out of the process. I guess he heard the Department was pretty strict about its uniform policy for rangers, as in "You really have to wear one." Then when he heard he might have to carry a firearm as a ranger, he was done. I was about to graduate with a double major in Geography and Environmental Studies, and it seemed ideal to me.

Mom, Dad; I PROMISE to get a job soon!
UC Santa Cruz graduation – June 1972

The application details are killing me; it's like death by a thousand paper cups...

A few months later I was in San Francisco at an interview. Although I knew absolutely nothing about the job of park ranger, I must have stumbled my way into a few answers that were good enough to land me on the civil service list. Later that summer, I was in New York visiting my brother, when Suzy called me, all excited. I had left Bob and Suzy as contacts in Santa Cruz with the Personnel Board, and they had heard from Sacramento that I might get hired that fall of '72. I worked my way quickly back to the west coast by early September. The personnel office at State Parks told me at that point that there would be two Ranger Trainee classes hired in the fall; one in September and one in December. I was positioned right between the two classes, but it was more likely that I would be at the top of the December group, so I was advised to hold tight for a few months. I found a place to live and found a job as a commercial fisherman. Then on Friday, September 15, I received a call from Dale Buschke in the personnel office. He said that one of the September class candidates had backed out at the last moment, so there was one job opening. The drawback was that I needed to be in Carlsbad the following Monday at 8 am! Talk about moving fast! I was not sure where Carlsbad was, but I did like caverns. I do remember thinking it kind of odd that a California State Park would be in New Mexico, but hey, it was the 70's and Jerry Brown would soon be elected Governor. Dale said he would interview me one more time before I was hired. Dale was on the road, so we agreed that we would meet in the San Jose airport on Saturday. We did the spy thing (I was wearing a brown sports coat with a red carnation) or something like that. Saturday morning I got a VERY SHORT haircut. Dale passed me on the final interview Saturday, but he told me I would need to get a haircut right away. Arghh! I got in my car and drove to Carlsbad, CALIFORNIA with all my worldly possessions (in an MGB) all day Sunday, and showed up for work on Monday needing a uniform, a haircut, and a place to live. Crazy times. Thank God for Marty Kania, who figured out immediately that my "deer in the headlights" look was for real and helped me deal with the scowls of Jack Welch and Frank Fairchild. She told me where to get a haircut and uniforms and how to find an apartment nearby. By Tuesday I was readier.

SAN DIEGO COAST

It is time to roll up our hands and get to work...

Jeff Price was my first supervisor – actually, technically a lead person I suppose. He was a great mentor, and we had some really good times together. One slow winter day on the beach of San Elijo, there was a little Scottie dog running loose. No one was around, so we decided to try to lasso him from the cab of the Ford Courier. One of us would drive, and the other try to get the pole with a loop of rope attached around the dog's neck. We never succeeded, and the dog's owner came up and read us the riot act. We deserved it, and he deserved the ticket for dog off leash. This was great training for the Anza-Borrego cattle capture fifteen years later, however.

Another trainee and I rented an apartment in Cardiff. I thought this was great, since I was assigned to San Elijo State Beach, only a couple blocks from the apartment. I would be able to walk to work, right past VG Donuts (which we called VD Donuts.) I think it is still there -- the donut shop, not the VD. The trouble was, I would be wearing a uniform on this walk, and I had to cross the railroad tracks next to the coast highway. There are millions of fist-sized rocks that make up the base for the railroad tracks, and the surfers found it fun to hurl these at me as I walked to work. I caught a ride home that afternoon, and drove to work thereafter.

My MGB got me to Carlsbad to begin my career at State Parks.

It stood out like a dog's sore thumb...

One sad story was the time a seasonal park aid named Ted collected a loose German Shepherd at Moonlight State Beach, a couple of miles up the Coast Highway from San Elijo. We would bring captured dogs back to San Elijo to a holding pen, and Animal Control would eventually come get them. So Ted tied the Shepherd up in the back of the Courier, and drove back to San Elijo through the town of Encinitas, where the official city motto at the time was "Death to Rangers!" Unfortunately, unbeknownst to the park aid, the Shepherd jumped out of the pickup right after they left Moonlight, and hanged himself off the side of the truck. So Ted dragged this poor dead dog through Encinitas and Cardiff and did not realize what had happened until he got to San Elijo. Actually, we did not have as many loose dog problems for the next few months.

One of the first things you learn as a ranger is that, when it comes to running campgrounds, the park aids RULE. Woe to the ranger that tries to help with the kiosk operation. I know park aids who would not take a break from the kiosk when certain rangers were their "relief" in the kiosk – it took too much effort to recover. My first night in the kiosk at the busy San Elijo campground, I assigned a LONG trailer to the "overflow" parking lot. We would try to accommodate campers without reservations by allowing them to spend one night in overflow; then they would have to leave early the next morning. I did not realize that the turning radius in overflow was about 3' 6", and once this poor guy with a trailer got into overflow, there was no way he was ever getting out. I think the State wound up purchasing his trailer, leaving it in place, and raffling it off to the park aid that could come up with the most creative way to reduce the "dog off leash" problem.

Fool me once, shame on you. Fool me, um...can't get fooled again!

Jeff taught me a few tricks in the kiosk. Campers would drive into campground and stop at the kiosk, or check station, to get their campsite assignment. When they made their reservation, they did not have to declare if they had a pet; we did that at the kiosk, since we would charge fees for dogs at that time. So when we asked them if they had any pets, the driver (always the husband –

always) would say one of two things: "Just the wife" or "Just the little monkeys in the back." Survey says: "Just the wife" 82% of the time. Gee, sir, never heard that one before. But Jeff reminded me that these people had been driving for a couple of hours and were tired, and our job was to help them have a good time. So we laughed uproariously each time like it was Jonathan Winters driving in, even though they seemed about as humorous as Spiro Agnew. The other trick was to try to get some clues about the campers as they drove up next to the kiosk window. Out-of-state license plates, parking decals, even the rare front bumper sticker (Divers Do It Deeper) would give us the opportunity to say something clever and show off our powers of ESPN. The best ever was the guy who was wearing a hard hat (no idea why) in the cab of his pickup, and he had a strip of Dymo tape on the front of the hard hat with his name on it. I guess that was so THE WIFE would not confuse it with her hard hat. Jeff, ever so smoothly, welcomed the driver by name before the guy said a word or handed us his reservation. His jaw dropped open, but we never told him our trick. (Since it worked well, it was now OUR trick; had it backfired....well, you get the picture.)

The shortest date I ever had with a nudist...

One of the most popular "off the beaten path" spots in San Diego was Black's Beach – an unofficial nude beach. It was city property, just south of and abutting Torrey Pines State Beach. Since it was unofficial, there was a lack of signs informing beach visitors of boundaries and policies. So a lot of nudes would wind up on the State Beach. We Rangers had what I thought was a reasonable policy about the nudes. We would approach them on foot patrol and inform them they had two options: they could move south on to Black's Beach if they really wanted to continue to sunbathe nude, or they could put on their swimsuits and stay at the State Beach. It was low key and it worked. One of the odd things I experienced during these contacts was that women, who one minute were on their backs naked, would almost invariably ask me to turn my back while they got dressed. I figured that it had to do with personal space – when they were naked, they were not threatened, but when a peace officer was standing there, it was more personal and more uncomfortable. I never turned my back totally, but I would "quarter" my stance so that I could keep them in my peripheral vision while not STARING right at them getting dressed – just enough of a turn to tell for sure if she were, um, let's say, a TRUE blonde. I would never turn my back on a naked bad guy or bad gal – you never knew what they might have hidden or where it might be stashed.

One afternoon I contacted a pair of women totally nude, lying on their backs on the State Beach and gave them the two options. They said they would move south, so I started walking over to the next group of nudes, when one of the women came running up to me, still naked. At first I thought, uh-oh, this is going to be a hassle, but then she asked me how she could become a park ranger. I told her that she would have to wear a uniform, but I don't think she got the humor. Having just gone through the hiring process myself, I was very familiar with it. After a few minutes of explaining detailed Personnel Board procedures, I asked her if she really wanted to be a ranger, and she said, "No, I just liked you and wanted to see if you would like to go out with me." Until then I had done a good job of "eyes above the neckline" and acting professionally, but I am sure I blushed very red at that point and started stammering. I was new in town and did not know anyone, so I said sure. Gee, I guess I never realized how sexy Personnel Board protocols could be…

!DO NOT INSERT PHOTOGRAPH OF NUDIST HERE!

If wifie shuns

Your fond embrace

Don't shoot the milkman

Shave your face

-- BURMA SHAVE

I picked her up at her apartment a few nights later (and yes, she was wearing clothes; that is probably why I did not recognize her and had to ask, "KitKat, is that you?") There was also a babysitter there, so I thought to myself this a night for several "firsts" -- my first date with a divorcee, first date with a mother, first date with a nudist, and, um, my first date with a true redhead. As I pulled away from the curb, she mentioned she had to be home kind of early – around 11 pm. I said that was fine, but why? She said "Well, my husband gets off work at 11:30 and gets home around midnight, so I really need to be home when he gets there." Yeah, no kidding. I pulled back to the curb and let her out. I swore off dating nudists right then and there. Total time of date: two minutes. I still wonder what she told the babysitter.

Put that in your hat and smoke it...

Part of our training was a trip to the District Six Office in downtown San Diego. Downtown has been revitalized in the past fifteen years, but in 1972 it was pretty rundown. Somehow, the State Building on Front Street got left off the revitalization plan. It was, and remains, a real dump – not exactly an inspiring location for Superintendent Jim Whitehead and his staff. Forty years later, I could see the State Building from the offices of The Nature Conservancy. I hope I never have to go inside that depressing building again. District Superintendent Jim Whitehead was a real inspiration, and a terrific public speaker and motivator. One of his quirks was his obsession on uniform perfection. He would dress you down if your shirt pockets were unbuttoned, your pen was standing slightly askew in your pocket, your hair was a little long, or (for women at the time) you were wearing unauthorized jewelry. However, these were all misdemeanors. The felony for a ranger was getting caught by Colonel Whitefeather (our fond local nickname) without your Stetson, or Smokey Bear hat, on.

Jim Whitehead and his attention to these details stuck with me. Ten years later, Jim had retired, and he would take long walks around Torrey Pines State Reserve and Los Penasquitos Lagoon. I was a resource ecologist at the time, and I also had projects at Torrey Pines. Dressed in civvies, I would be at Torrey Pines and see Jim walk by, and I would automatically reach for my shirt pockets to see if they were buttoned. That man had some influence! Later, as a District Superintendent, I was also fierce about ensuring that Rangers wore their Stetsons on duty.

His sweat hit the floor of the classroom in one swell foop...

During the "Ranger Trainee" program, we would go to Asilomar for part of our training, and to a criminal justice center in Modesto for the law enforcement portion of our training. The training was interspersed with field experience, unlike the six month academy that cadets go to now. Our law enforcement academy in Modesto was only five weeks long, and classes were taught by local police officers, deputies, and Highway Patrolmen. Modesto is really hot in the spring, when we were there. One of our favorite instructors was a sergeant named Bobby Joe Billy Bob Farr, and ol' Bobby must have weighed about three hundred pounds. I am guessing he did not qualify for the physical fitness bonus every year. He would wear polyester shirts, and even during just a one hour class, ol' BJBB would start to sweat something fierce. Dick Troy, Ray Patton, Dan Preece and I would entertain ourselves by having a betting pool on the exact time the first drop of sweat would fall off the end of his sleeve on to the floor. I cannot imagine what we would have cooked up in a six month academy.

There were some really creative ranger-trainees at San Diego Coast. Terry Brann and I cooked up the idea of establishing a Hike and Bike campground at San Elijo State Beach. Again, there were a lot of people travelling up and down the coast of California, by bicycle or other means, and we figured we could help put some of them up legally at the State Beach. One added benefit of the Hike and Bike site was that we also used it for the campfire center, which previously had been in the parking lot – a very busy and unfriendly location. This new campground, which held about a dozen people, was developed and served several purposes.

The needle is on empty; if we get there we'll be breathing fumes...

We all probably do a few dumb things during our careers. One of mine took place at Torrey Pines State Reserve during my trainee year. It is hard to believe now during these very lean and difficult times at State Parks, but we actually had way too many staff in 1972/73 at the "Intake Areas". Trainees were assigned to Intake Areas, of which San Diego Coast in Carlsbad was one. The trainees were there in addition to the regular staff, so there were a bunch of permanents, seasonals, and trainees running over the same ground.

17

They decimated our seasonal funds by 15%!

I was assigned to night patrol at Torrey Pines State Reserve, which was open for day use only. So my job was really that of night watchman – to make sure no one entered the Reserve at night. It was also important to try NOT to be on duty for the lifeguard parties at the Reserve. You did NOT want to be the only Ranger on duty during these parties, and you DID want to be at the party. They were soon banned by management. The official reason for banning them was that "They got too gnarly." Hey, it was San Diego in the early 70's. I knew we should have invited the managers to the party.

Anyway, on a typical night, I would break up the evening by taking hikes through the Reserve along with the vehicle patrols of the half-vast (1.1 miles) road network. There was a gate at the Reserve entrance, and it was partway up a hill. Below the gate was a berm, then the beach, then the Pacific Ocean. One night I got lazy while opening the locked gate, and left the "manual transmission" Jeep in which I was patrolling running in neutral with the parking brake on. Just as I was putting the key in the gate's lock, I heard a pop and saw the Jeep rolling backwards towards the ocean. It was one of those moments when the consequences of your actions are crystal clear (Jeep sinks in ocean; I get fired in year one) and they are contrasted with the consequences of a distinct action (jump in Jeep and possibly get seriously injured or killed). I immediately jumped in the Jeep, jammed on the brakes, passed through the gate, this time using the right procedures, and took a very long hike in the Reserve.

Although San Diego Coast and its complement of beach campgrounds, day use beaches, and Torrey Pines did not exactly match up to my fantasy of patrolling large redwoods parks (like Denzil did!), there were good options nearby.

Anza-Borrego Desert and Cuyamaca Rancho State Parks were an hour or two away, and a couple of the Trainees at San Diego Coast that I had gotten to know in earlier training groups were now assigned to Anza-Borrego. So I started going out to the desert for ride-alongs. It was so different from the coastal parks – almost 600,000 acres of beautiful desert and mountains, and the job was totally different. The job seemed to be one that I had more in mind when I signed on – backcountry patrol, search and rescue, and resource management. The downside was obviously the heat, but the rangers seemed to embrace the challenges of dealing with the extreme summers. Their patrol vehicles had no air conditioning at the time, and they would take the doors off their CJ-5's as a means of keeping cool. At Asilomar, when our training group would be together, I would talk about Anza-Borrego as a great place to be assigned, and the consensus was "Be careful what you ask for." I never did get to work at the desert as a ranger, but later was assigned there as a Superintendent. Plus, during my time as a resource ecologist, I spent a significant amount of effort at the park.

PENDLETON COAST

After nine months as a Trainee, the Department started placing us in our first permanent assignments. As I mentioned, the Intake Areas were overstaffed, and the summer season was about to begin, so we were farmed out. My best friend in our Trainee Class was a fellow named Dick Troy, whose Intake Area was the Santa Cruz Mountains. Dick and I were both assigned to Doheny State Beach as our first permanent jobs. It was not particularly exciting to either of us, but we knew we could make it work.

Nothing has ever ceased to amaze me…

Our first day was a real eye opener. Now remember, Dick and I had just come out of the Ranger Training Program, where you are taught the correct procedures and policies for all aspects of the Visitor Services function (all except parking Jeeps on hills!). So the first morning, the Park Supervisor wanted to show us how to make a bank drop of the park weekend revenues. So he went to the safe, grabbed the weekend cash intake of about $3,000, and put it in a cloth sack. Then on the way to the bank, we stopped by the local coffee shop for a cup of coffee. The Supervisor put the cash on a table, placed his Stetson hat on top of the cash (for security, I guess), and led us up to the counter to place our order. Dick and I had our eyes glued on the cash the whole time, as I recall.

When we got back to the office, the Supervisor bragged to us about the very recent installation of a $60,000 Public Address system for the whole State Beach – day use and campground area. He said our jobs would be so easy, since we really did not have to leave the office to make contacts anymore; we could just use the PA system. Again, this did not match well with our recent training. Can you imagine – some poor schmo is dumb enough to violate a park regulation (say, no gloves in the glove box) – and all of a sudden he hears on the PA, "Sir, yes YOU in the pink Maverick wearing the bad toupee...." I don't think either Dick or I ever used the PA system once to make a personal contact. Shades of M.A.S.H. or Big Brother.

That's the proverbial problem with overcrowding in Parks; it's like trying to stuff three pounds of candy into a four – pound bag...

The stupidest policy ever at Doheny was regarding the use of the large lawns in the day use area. The unit policy was that these large grassy, mowed lawns were off limits to organized games and sports. Let's see, a large lawn at a beach in southern California, and visitors could not really use it to play on. Could someone explain to me why the park designers put these stupid lawns here then? When asked the reason for the policy, the Park Supervisor said that the maintenance staff complained that all the public activity on the lawns would wear out the grass. I spent a lot of time on weekend afternoons kicking out groups of soccer, badminton, volleyball, and softball players. It is hard enough sometimes to gain public compliance with park rules that make sense. When the rules or policies are really dumb, it makes for long, difficult afternoons. Apparently, the ideals of public service taught by Jim Whitehead at Asilomar did not always survive their long trek down the chain of command to some field supervisors.

Friends would visit me at Doheny State Beach, but we
could not play games on the lawns – only on the beach.

He really stepped over the third rail with that comment...

Dick and I were probably typical of young rookie Rangers. We
were optimistic, innocent, energetic, and anxious to try out new
ideas. Fresh from interpretation training, we convinced the Park
Supervisor and the Maintenance Supervisor that the maintenance
staff could become involved in our interpretive programs. We
should have been more wary, since Buster, the Maintenance
Supervisor who "volunteered" to do a campfire program, was the
same fellow who hated seeing visitors having fun on our lawns.

He created a slide show, and Dick and I agreed to do the warm-up for the campfire program. After our silly songs and skits, the campers were ready to be inspired. Buster then launched into his program of "before and after" slides. "Here is a shot of our restrooms on Friday afternoon, nice and clean, before YOU people show up. Now here is a shot of that same restroom on Sunday afternoon after YOU have had forty-eight hours to trash it." This went on and on. Unfortunately, the District Interpretive Specialist, Dom Gotelli, had picked that evening, unannounced, to review our campfire program. After what seemed an eternity of Buster's talk, Dom stood up, slammed his folding chair closed, and left. He was soon followed out by almost every camper. At least Dick and I did not have to cut off the program short.

I credit Dick and Jeff Price with getting me over my fear of public speaking, or, in this case, my fear of acting like an idiot in public. Campfire programs really cure you of stage fright, because you have to get up and sing silly songs and do skits in front of teenaged boys and their parents, who are often at least a little looped. Most of the audience is there to have fun, and they enjoy seeing the rangers act semi-human.

We could stand here and talk until the cows turn blue, or we could DO something...

Either rangers were bolder "back in the day" or I was really naïve. When Dick and I were assigned to San Onofre State Beach, we pretty much put in a walk-in campground with very little management input and absolutely without the knowledge of anyone in Sacramento. We took an active (behind the scenes) role in fighting the expansion of the San Onofre Nuclear Generating Station into the park, and organized a stakeout for "car clouts" that ended in the Area Manager's personal Porsche being broken into. It was kind of funny in a way that the Area Manager then jumped into his own Porsche with a broken window and helped chased down the bad guys.

We also created, very much tongue in cheek, the "Save the Haplopappus League." In the early 70's, it seemed like a support group was being created for every mega-charismatic macrovertebrate (Save the Whales!) We felt sorry for the underappreciated, and less than spectacular, *Haplopappus*.

Come to think of it, I have not received my copy of "The Happy Haplo" newsletter for quite some time now…

MOUNT SAN JACINTO STATE PARK

You shouldn't put all your eggs in one basket; but what if you only have one egg...

In the early 70's, the transfer policy was, let us say, not quite as fair as it is now. Transfers were left up to the discretion of the District Superintendents and the Personnel Office in Sacramento. After less than a year at Doheny and San Onofre (Pendleton Coast District at the time), I was itching to get assigned to a state park rather than a busy recreation area. A unique job at Mt. San Jacinto State Park became open – a wilderness ranger at the top of the Palm Springs Aerial Tramway. The Department wanted the ranger to live at the top of the tramway, so it did not appeal to a lot of people. It was remote, and you had to rely on the tramway schedule for transportation (unless you wanted to hike fifteen miles out to Idyllwild). So I applied, and soon received a call from District Superintendent Jim Whitehead, who told me I had been selected as the best candidate. When I asked how many applicants there were, he said I was the only one. So technically, I was also the worst applicant. Ah well. You takes your victories where and when you can, and I was going to a real park!

The ranger station I would be living in was at an elevation of 8400'. The tramway went from the desert near Palm Springs to Long Valley, so the changes in temperature and elevation were extreme. In the winter, the desert would have warm days, while Mt. San Jacinto could have a snowstorm at the same time. It made for quite a challenge when visitors would show up in shorts and sandals and want to take a long hike into the wilderness. There was a permit system in place that required everyone entering the wilderness, whether for day use or camping, to obtain a permit. This allowed the park staff to monitor and control wilderness carrying capacities. More importantly, it allowed us to contact directly most of the people entering the wilderness and help them make good decisions about how to spend what could turn out to be their last hours of life. I found the best technique for dissuading people was to personalize the decision from my point of view. "Gee, sir: I live and work here, and hike or ski over ten miles every day at this altitude, and have every safety gizmo known to humankind, and know every inch of this here mountain, and there is NO WAY I would go into the wilderness today with that huge winter storm coming in." I never told them that THEY would not make it; just that I would not. That invariably worked.

It's as plain as the egg on your face...

The tramway ran from about ten a.m. to nine p.m., so it was rare to have visitors at night. All the wilderness camping began about two miles from the ranger station. When I first moved into the ranger station, I wanted to see if my body would adjust to the harsh conditions. So I avoided using chapstick and lotions that would ease my transition to a very dry climate and increased sun exposure. I was doing pretty well for a while, I thought. One summer night, though, I decided to sleep outside, on the deck of the ranger station, in a light sleeping bag. I was surprised early the next morning when a backpacker came to the ranger station to ask questions, since he would have had to start hiking really early (or else he camped illegally nearby.) I got out of the sleeping bag, and we both went inside the ranger station. I got him a map, answered a few questions, and we must have chatted for at least ten minutes. Finally he took off, and I went into the bathroom. I looked in the mirror, and saw that my lip had split badly in the night, and one side of my face was totally caked in dried blood. The camper had not said a word! I guess we were even, since I had not mentioned his really offensive body odor.

At least when my parents visited, they were prepared (note the jackets and ski poles!) Dad would have preferred a golf club.

My parents liked to visit me at San Jacinto, and one day we went for a day hike up to Round Valley, about two miles away from the Long Valley Ranger Station. My mom was fascinated by the storage shed in Round Valley, because one of the entrance doors was about twelve feet off the ground. There were no ladders or ropes around, so she wondered what that door was for. I told her I would show her later. When we got back to Long Valley, I pulled out a picture of twelve-foot snowdrifts at the storage shed. The upper door was the only way to get in without digging out a WHOLE LOT of snow. In an emergency, the ability to access the storage shed through the upper door could become invaluable.

He's one of those guys who has grown up with his own bootstraps...

I would say that the person who had the greatest impact on my career was the Supervising Ranger at Mt. San Jacinto – Jerry Henderson. We hit it off right away and became good friends. Unfortunately, Jerry did not stay in the Department too long. I don't think the Department could keep up with his high energy, big thinking, and his ambition.

I think we got along like a house gathering no moss...

Although Jerry was only five years older than I, it felt like more. He was married, had children, and had been a Captain in the US Marines in Vietnam. He was also going to UC Riverside at night, pursuing a master's in public administration. In short, I was a boy and Jerry was a man. My world seemed pretty tame compared to his. Plus, I was still kind of shy and quiet. But Jerry's greatest lesson for me was how to "go after it". I was complaining one day that I was never selected for advanced interpretation training, and Jerry asked me what I had done to be selected. I told him I had submitted my name when the notice was sent around. He just stared at me, like he was saying, "And that's it?" He proceeded to tell me that if you want something in life, you have to go after it. You cannot sit back and expect the Department, or any person or entity, to hand you something, even if you deserve it. You have to bang on doors, break down barriers, set goals, and figure out how to achieve them. And when you get knocked off the rails, you have to figure out how to get back on and succeed the next time. This was a great life lesson that has served me well ever since, although there were probably at least a few subsequent supervisors that wished I had remained quiet and shy.

Jerry and I had a terrific time hiking, skiing, and snowshoeing together. We also had good discussions about park philosophy and park management. During Jerry's tenure on the mountain, that state park undoubtedly went through the greatest changes in management it ever has experienced or ever will endure. Trails were re-routed for resource management purposes, a permit system was instituted, open fires were banned, the concept of wilderness campsites away from meadows was instituted, and carrying capacities for camping were established. Jerry showed outstanding leadership, and he was quick to give credit to others if they had better ideas!

I will miss seeing him around the shoehorn…

Jerry also had one of those "larger than life" personalities. He had a huge smile and a loud distinctive laugh. Outgoing and friendly, he was a wonderful ambassador for the park. Campfire programs were so fun in the wilderness. These would be wilderness campers, and we would have a campfire every Saturday night in the summer. But when Jerry would lead a song, it would create chaos. He was a great song leader and full of personality, although he had no idea how to keep the beat. He would lead a song and get everyone clapping, but the campers would be confused about whether to clap with Jerry or clap to the beat of the song. It added to the hilarity of the evening.

You can't let all of your eggs out of the basket at once…

One of our park aids started dating a woman who worked for the Forest Service in one of the fire lookout towers near the town of Idyllwild, a dozen or so miles from the Tramway mountain station. Mike would hike up to Strawberry Divide at night, from where he had a direct line of sight to the Tahquitz lookout tower. He and his honey would send Morse code signals to each other by flashlight, which was pretty cool. "Oh Baby, I really want to …. ..- --. you tonight." (Gee, I hope I did that right!) She also wrote a weekly column for the Idyllwild newspaper, and she would chronicle the progress of their romance over the course of the summer. It gave new meaning to "I'm going to go behind that tree and flash my girlfriend now." I guess today they would call, text, toot, or tweet each other, but their method of canoodlin' seemed more romantic back then.

I would hike to Strawberry Divide in the hopes
of meeting a canoodler, always without luck.

The park headquarters was in Idyllwild, along with the "old school"
Area Manager, a ranger, and two campgrounds. The ranger,
Herb, had a funny story about when he first started working there.
One of the jobs was to clean the bathrooms in the campgrounds
every morning. Herb figured that was his duty, so his first morning
he grabbed the cleaning supplies at eight a.m. and headed for the
toilets. When he got there, he discovered that they had already
been cleaned by Bill, the Area Manager. Herb thought that it
wasn't right for the boss to have to clean toilets, so he came in at
seven a.m. the next day and was able to clean the toilets. The
third day, he came in again at seven, but now the toilets had
already been cleaned by Bill. Herb cleaned the toilets at six a.m.
on the fourth day, but on the fifth day, when he came in at six, he
found – yup -- clean toilets. Herb decided that Bill really wanted to
clean the toilets, and Herb really did not want to get up any earlier,
so the problem was solved.

Finally the other shoes are beginning to drop into place...

If it were close to a full moon, after the campfire program a couple of the park aids would lead a night hike to Mt. San Jacinto peak, 10,831' in elevation. This was a commitment for the campers, since it was a seven mile round trip hike in the dark and an elevation gain of almost two thousand feet. Everyone that ever went on the hike described it as fantastic, so we kept doing it. The park aids would sometimes lead the hike barefoot (them, not the campers)! I cannot imagine a supervisor allowing hikes like these in this day and age of liability awareness. Maybe barefoot moonlight hikes should be required at management seminars.

As I mentioned, if you lived at the Long Valley Ranger Station, as I did, your transportation up and down the mountain was at the mercy of the tram schedule. I was surprised by how many people asked me if I went backpacking on my days off. Although I was in the best shape of my life, I would want to do something different on my days off. My joke was that I would go into the city to get away from it all.

Since it was southern California, home of many amusement parks, and based on how the tram board marketed the tramway ride (Welcome to Tramwayland!), most visitors would assume it was a controlled environment at the top – measured hikes that were totally safe. As mentioned before, that made the visit to the park more riskier, since many visitors assumed there was no danger. But the minute the sun went down, especially after a warm spring or fall day, it got cold very fast, and unprepared day hikers were often in trouble right away. In addition, the park loomed over Palm Springs and the Coachella Valley, where warm winters drew "snowbirds" and lots of day visitors from all over southern California. Our favorite visitors were those dressed for a day in the valley, where it was probably eighty degrees. They would ascend the mountain in the tram, and then want to take a hike. Again, it would be pleasant, around sixty degrees in Long Valley, and they would go hiking, sometimes even in high heels. We had a lot of close calls up there, and several visitor fatalities in the winters. It is a beautiful wilderness area, and thousands of visitors enjoy it in the winter, since the tram eliminates traffic jams and the need to put on chains.

There has always existed a certain level of tension between the tramway and the state park. The tramway wants as many people as possible to ride the tram up to the mountain station. Except for gift shop and restaurant sales, the tram tickets account for their revenues. On the other hand, the state park staff has to deal with the thousands of people who ride the tram up to the edge of the wilderness. Granted, a lot of visitors do not even leave the mountain station. Long Valley, a beautiful forest valley next to the mountain station of the tram, serves as a buffer area. There is a stream running through the valley, and tram riders can hike and picnic in Long Valley without a wilderness permit. This valley creates a lot of conflict, because the tramway authority wants to create more attractions there for visitors. As mentioned above, the main problem arises when people who are unprepared for the wilderness enter the wilderness anyway.

To get to my home in the Long Valley Ranger Station, I had to rely on the tramway to get up and down the mountain. Actually, I could hike in from Idyllwild (a fifteen mile, all day hike) or climb up Chino Canyon, the canyon that the tramway also ascends. Jerry and I tackled this canyon once, and it was a long, difficult, but immensely enjoyable hike/climb.

The last tram up the mountain to get me home left the valley at nine p.m., so if I were on a date or out with friends, I would really have to call it quits early. I was reminded of this years later when Jim Burke and his family moved to Cuyamaca Rancho State Park. Jim had just left Angel Island, where he had to rely on the schedule of the ferry between the mainland and the island. Jim said that when they first moved to Cuyamaca, he and his wife had a couple of panicky moments when they would be, say, shopping in El Cajon, look at their watches, and think "We are going to miss the ferry – RUN!" Then they would remember that they could actually take their time; Jim could go back to shopping for more vintage copies of "MAD" magazine before they had to drive home.

We were taught, as rangers, that "command presence" was important. The idea there was that, in every contact with a visitor or group, that you should retain control of the situation, and the best way to maintain control was to act respectfully towards the visitor and ensure that they treated you respectfully. I had to use command presence one night at the very top of Mt. San Jacinto.

In the 70's, it was legal to camp at the peak, as long as you possessed a camping permit for the peak, although camping is no longer allowed at the peak. There were some terrific campsites nestled among the boulders and limber pines found up there. It was great to camp at nearly eleven thousand feet elevation, snuggle into your sleeping bag, watch the stars, feel your lips bleeding, and listen to the wind. Almost always, you had the place to yourself at night due to the elevation, lack of water, and often harsh conditions.

I hope there will be a silver lining at the end of the rainbow for both of them…

So one night I was sleeping up there, and it was pretty late, when I awoke to hear a couple of guys arrive and start to make camp. They undoubtedly thought no one else was around, since they were banging pots and pans around and making no attempt to be quiet, and my campsite was pretty concealed. I kept thinking they would soon go to sleep and I could deal with them in the morning. But they sat around and kept talking loudly. I was tired, and I just did not have it in me to get fully dressed, so I just walked over to their campsite wearing nothing but my boxers and carrying nothing but a flashlight. Probably not the greatest policing technique. I announced myself as the ranger and asked to see their camping permit, and they handed me their day use permit. I mentioned that their permit was not valid for camping, and they responded that the park ranger in Idyllwild told them that if they hiked to the peak and there was no one else there, it would be okay for them to camp there. I asked if they had talked to the ranger cleaning toilets in the bathroom around five a.m., but they did not understand. So I told them that no park ranger would tell them that, and that there WERE actually other people camping legally at the peak that night. I told them to pack up their gear and hike back to Idyllwild since their permit was for day-use only. They did not say another word and packed up and left.

I suspect they had a pretty good story to tell about getting rousted by a ranger in his underwear. My memory is getting poor, so I do not recall if those were my boxers covered with the red hearts, the skiing penguins, or the tramway logo.

A hike to the peak, mid-80's. San Jacinto was the only park where I worked as a ranger, park ecologist, and superintendent.

It looks like they let one of the chickens into the henhouse...

One of the weirdest arrests I ever made was at Mt. San Jacinto. I was living in the ranger station at the top of the tram, in Long Valley. Since it was in the middle of a busy public use area, I usually left the park on my days off. But one day I was at home, off duty, when there was a frantic pounding on the front door of the ranger station. I ran out front, and it was Janine, one of the tramway ticket booth employees. She told me she and a female friend had been hiking, and after a snack had split up for a while. While separated, a male had approached her friend, and, at knifepoint, forced her to copulate him orally. I asked where her friend and the assailant were, and she said her friend was back at the mountain station, trying to catch the next tram down to the valley. We went up to the mountain station and found her friend. I asked her if she knew where the assailant had gone, and she exclaimed, "That's him getting on the tram car right now"!

I was in casual dress, so I told the victim to stay on the mountain until the next tram car. I told the car operator to call the Palm Springs police, and to run the car as slowly as possible to give the police a chance to get to the valley station before we arrived. And I got on the tram car. This was in the days before all rangers carried firearms, and Mt. San Jacinto was not one of the parks that had authorized firearms yet. So if things got dicey, my only real option was to climb out through the window of the tram car and slide down the cables.

I knew that he probably still had a knife with him, so I kept a low profile and acted like a regular tourist – that's right: drunk and wearing clothes that looked like they were made from Motel 6 shower curtains. Fortunately, the police were waiting at the valley station, and we arrested him when he exited the tram car. It turns out he was sixteen and was currently in a half-way house for juvenile criminals. This was one of their "supervised" field trips. Supervised by whom, I wondered.

At his trial for the sexual assault, once I testified, I had to leave the court, since the records of juvenile proceedings are kept confidential. Naturally, I was interested in the outcome. As the District Attorney came out of the courtroom, I asked him how it had gone. He told me he could not tell me, of course. But then he added, "But if someone else were to walk by and tell you that the kid had been found guilty, if I were you, I would believe that person." Pretty clever, I thought.

SANTA CRUZ MOUNTAINS

In 1976 I transferred to Henry Cowell Redwoods State Park. I was lucky there to work with a couple of the greatest backup rangers in the state – Steve Treanor and Ed Tavares. If you ever needed help, they were right there, ready for business. At the time, Cowell was a wild place, and we called upon each other for backup often. In my two years there, at least nine murders were committed in the park. Drug use, nudity, theft, resource destruction, violence, and hatred for law enforcement officers were rampant. After having gone to college right next door, and having transferred from the relatively mild Mt. San Jacinto State Park, it was quite a change for me.

A family visit to Big Basin in 1956
(my brother Roger, me, my mother)

I wouldn't be caught dead there with a ten-foot pole…

Every afternoon in the summer, my partner and I would take a hike down the length of the San Lorenzo River that ran through the park. "The Gorge" was the hotbed for illegal activity. We would wear "mesh" boots on this hike that would allow water to drain out of the boots. The reason was that, although the river ran all year, it was usually less than three feet deep in the summer. So we would be on one side of the river and make a contact with some bad guys on the other side of the river. They invariably had a sense of protection, since they thought the river provided a barrier between us and them. I loved the way they would give us a bunch of lip, and then become astounded as we walked right through the river to give them citations or arrest them. Some of them would quote the Bible, or perhaps it was Woody Allen, and tell me to "Be Fruitful and Multiply", but not in those exact words.

It took more than one language to ensure
that visitors had no fun in the parks!

At first, I would try to be a nice guy (well, semi-nice) and only write a citation to the person whom I perceived to be the leader of the bad guys. Then, invariably, one of his brilliant companions would ask, "Hey, why are you picking on Joe and not writing us ALL tickets?" That is where I would say, "Great question, Einstein. Let's see ID's for all of you" and I would gladly accommodate their request for greater fairness in this world.

We needed to get out the vacuum cleaner and hose this guy down...

Henry Cowell Redwoods State Park was next to the community of Felton, and 100% of the residents of Felton owned large dogs and enjoyed letting them run loose in the park. That sounded fun, but rangers had to clean up a lot of deer that had been killed by packs of loose dogs. So there was a pretty constant battle over the issue of loose dogs. I kept trying to recruit park aid Ted from Moonlight State Beach, without success. It was hard to catch loose dogs, but when you found the owner WITH their dogs in the park, it was pretty automatic that you would write a citation. One day I saw two loose German Shepherds bouncing around the picnic area, and sure enough they were next to a young gentleman who appeared to spend, oh, about twelve hours every day lifting weights. The contact started off poorly, since when I asked him for ID, he literally flung it at my chest. I caught it somehow and started writing a ticket to Mr. Paul LeDoux for dogs off leash in a state park. I called Steve and Ed for backup, and the fun began. They arrived just as I was finishing up writing the citation. I handed the bad guy my pen so that he could sign the ticket, and he theatrically dropped the pen on the ground. So Paul LeDoux and I began our pas-de-deux. He said "I can't sign; I don't have a pen." He was angry and built like a shit brickhouse. And he had two large Shepherds who were looking very hungry and gnarly. On my side, I had Ed and Steve and three ever-so-reliable .38 caliber Dan Wesson revolvers. I calmly laid out the options. "Now Paul, this can go one of two ways, and it is TOTALLY up to you. Here is the first option: you are currently under arrest. If you sign this citation, I will release you from arrest, since you are promising to appear in court and resolve this matter. You will leash your dogs and we will part ways. Here is the second option: you are currently under arrest, yet you might not sign the citation, which is telling me that you are refusing to appear in court and resolve this matter. In that case, I will place you in handcuffs and transport you to the county lockup, where you will be booked into jail. You will be given the opportunity to post bail and be released. In order to post bail, you must promise to appear in court and resolve this matter. If you then do not appear in court, you will forfeit bail and a bench warrant will be issued for your arrest. Further, my partners and I fear that your loose dogs may run down and kill a deer, so we are going to have to deal with them after you leave for the hoosegow. And we have a boss who has told us to use ANY means necessary to deal with this issue. So, Paul, what's it going to be?"

Don't look at me in that tone of voice...

For what seemed like a very long time, Paul and I glared at each other. In fact, it was the worst glaring contest I had had since I was a teenager, and I belched at the dinner table really loudly. My mother asked me if I would do that if the Queen of England were having dinner with us, and I responded that if the Queen were seated here, I hoped we would be having a much better dinner. In my fantasy world, I imagined that she would laugh so hard at my cleverness that I would avoid punishment. I was proven wrong. My mother called it her "middle-aged housewife's glare." I was not sure what to call my glare, but it was not THAT.

Anyway, Paul eventually picked up the pen off the ground ever so slowly and signed the citation. So, I had won exactly fifty percent of the glaring contests in my life. I checked to be sure he did not sign "Mickey Mouse" or use some other clever alias, and he leashed his dogs and left. Man, those French guys were tough…

These guys are a regular Rhodes gallery of crooks…

One day I was in the office by the entrance station when we got a call from the Sheriff's office. They told us that a grand theft auto had just taken place in Felton. Four African-American juveniles had stolen a '68 white Cadillac convertible from the local barber and were now somewhere in the vicinity. I looked up, and driving into the park was a '68 white Cadillac convertible with the top down with four…yup. Of course, I could not be sure it was the same Cadillac. Two of the bad guys were sitting on the back deck of the convertible with their legs in the back seat, probably to avoid drawing attention to themselves. I told the Sheriff to send backup right away and then ran out to stop them; they took one look at me and turned down a service road. The Sheriff came down the service road from the opposite direction; we had them penned in. They took one look at him, and decided to take their chances with me. It was a pretty easy felony bust.

The bad guys said that they had been in the local barber shop and asked the barber whose Cadillac was parked outside. When the barber said that it was his, they asked where the keys were. The barber, NATURALLY, retrieved the car keys. One of the bad guys asked the barber to put the keys in his own palm and keep his palm face up. Then he bet him a whole dollar that he could grab the keys before the barber could close his fist. And how did that work out for you, Mr. Barber? Gee, maybe the barber deserved to lose his Cadillac. At least the barber never paid off the bet; well, I am assuming that he never did…

I got to feed the deer at Big Basin Redwoods State Park in the summer of 1956. Feeding deer was prohibited by park management a few years later. I wound up working at Rancho del Oso, part of Big Basin Redwoods SP, as a ranger in the mid-1970's. My duties included, well, you guessed it...

"I always knew that, due to all the sports and activities I participated in, I would wind up old and decrepit. I just never figured this would take place while I was still young."

--- The Author

Illegally feeding the wildlife must have been genetic, because my
grandmother was caught on camera feeding a bear in
Yellowstone National Park on her honeymoon.
I cannot believe she survived this incident.

They needed to get all their ducks into one sock...

I still don't know how Ed sniffed this next incident out. It was the
off-season, so rangers would put down their donuts long enough
to go out to the kiosk from the office to collect fees when the
occasional car would drive into the day use area. So Ed and I

were in the office, a couple of cars drove in, and Ed went out to collect the day use fees. A minute later, Ed came back in the office and asked me what I thought of this situation: both cars were driven by a juvenile male, and there was a juvenile female in each car. However, rather than sit in the usual passenger seat, each girl was sitting in the back seat directly behind the driver. I said I had no idea what to make of it. But Ed said it was a dead giveaway that they had beer in the trunk. Well, of course! We snuck over to the day use parking lot to spy on them, and sure enough – all four kids went over to the open trunk of one of the cars and took out a case of beer to carry into the picnic area. I still don't get it and suspect that Ed never told me the whole story, but we did pour out a whole lot of beer that day. Part of me still suspects that Ed had a couple of his high school buddies play a trick on me. Part of why I think Ed set me up is that he got so angry when I insisted on pouring out all four cases of beer. He kept arguing we should keep the beer and make the kids' parents come pick it up at the office. I kept pouring. You could always tell when Ed was excited about something – his neck muscles would pop out like thick rope; his jaw would thrust forward, and his eyes would get squinty. Man, was I was glad that he was on my side. Even when he was angry with me, I think he was still on my side.

After an exchange of gunfire between the cops, the suspect was arrested...

We started to have a rash of thefts in the campground. Usually, some campers would take a day hike, and when they came back to their campsite, their motor home, trailer, or tent had been broken into, and several items would be missing. Usually, it was food or small camping gear, but there was one incident where a green Kelty backpack and a twelve-gauge shotgun were reported stolen. We suspected that someone was camping or living nearby illegally and keeping an eye on campers' activities.

One day a couple of rangers found an illegal campsite near the campground, and there was a man camping there. They pulled his driver's license and told him to stay there while they looked around (Yeah, right!) Unfortunately, they took their eyes off him, and he boogied. But they did have his license, and we knew what type of stolen gear he still might have with him, including the backpack and the shotgun.

Some days later, I was driving on Highway 1 through the town of Santa Cruz, and I saw a man hitchhiking with his back to traffic. He was wearing a green Kelty. I slowed down as I passed him and got a look at his face, and it was the same guy whose driver's license had been pulled and circulated. Highway 1 soon changed from a freeway to a surface street, so I drove on ahead and parked on the street. We arrested the bad guy, and he was later convicted. The whole case rested on the legality of the search of his backpack, because in the backpack was the shotgun, which he had sawn off ("to shoot rabbits", he told me.) It matched the one reported stolen, so it was a good connection to the thefts. In Dan Friend's book, Confessions of the Night Ranger, he relates the details of this arrest on the streets of Santa Cruz, along with some of the angst on the part of many rangers at the time about when to draw your weapon.

Is it the "N" or the "Zero"; what part of N-O do you not understand…

Rangers make a lot of visitor contacts for littering, but it is rare to book a litterer into County jail. In fact, today, the jail would probably not make this booking. In a separate instance, we were again experiencing a lot of campground thefts. Every time I would see this one bad guy in the campground, there would be one or two reported thefts that evening or the next day. But I could never catch him, despite staking out the campground at night on many occasions. But in my mind, it was clear that he was the thief. So one day I confronted him and told him he had to leave the campground and that he was never allowed back in. This was totally a bluff, since there was no legal basis to kick him out. Anyway, the next day, the little idiot was walking through the campground drinking a bottle of beer. He saw me, kind of panicked, and threw the beer bottle into the woods right in front of me. Now I had him on a misdemeanor committed in my presence. So I arrested and cuffed him and hauled him to jail.

The Sheriff ran a records check on him, and all of a sudden we were getting a rap sheet five pages long. Same first, middle, and last names, and same date of birth (DOB). The only thing wrong was that the guy I arrested was about 5'8" and 140 pounds, and the rap sheet was for a much taller and heavier guy. We finally concluded there were two idiots with the same name and DOB.

When the deputy was putting him into a cell, the bad guy got really stupid and got into a physical fight with the deputy. That earned him an extra six months in County lockup. I can just picture the jailhouse talk. "Smitty – What are you in for?" "Burglary; four months." "Jonesy – How about you?" "Assault and battery; five months." "What about you, Genius?" "Um, littering in a state park; six months!" Stunned silence. Furthermore, you know what they say about how child molesters and park litterers are treated by other prisoners...

A loose tongue spoils the broth...

One day I was patrolling with Steve Treanor, and we were driving into the park through the day use entrance, which goes through a meadow. Steve suddenly stopped the truck and pointed to the middle of the meadow. There you could see, well, two bare cheeks rising rhythmically into the air. We walked over to the site and asked the couple to get dressed. She had a great response – "Are you really going to arrest us for being in love?" Steve just nodded and kept writing the citation. I kept thinking perhaps we were letting them off easy; what if they were litterers as well?

GAVIOTA and UC SANTA BARBARA

This place is hanging over my head like a bad penny...

After having been a ranger for six years, I started wondering if there were other opportunities within the Department for me. Also, I was having doubts whether orbiting campgrounds and making hundreds of contacts for dog off leash and third vehicle in the campsite was really my life work. About the same time, the Department was expanding its role in resource management – the care and protection of the natural resources it held in public trust. To that end, the Department decided it needed more professional resource managers in-house to guide that management and protection effort. So it started to expand the role and number of resource managers on staff. Up until this point, around 1977, the few positions in the Department in the professional resource field were in Sacramento and were classified as forester, wildlife manager, and the like. In the late-70's, the Department created the Resource Ecologist series, expanded the role to provide more generalized expertise, and placed six of these positions in the District offices.

This type of position strongly appealed to me, so I started to plan a career change AND stay in the Department. At that time, the Department would consider helping to fund educational opportunities. With a degree in Geography, I started to look at the UC and CSU campuses that offered a master's in that discipline. It became clear that Berkeley, Santa Barbara, and UCLA had the best Geography departments, and that UCSB had the program and classes that fit my interests most closely. So I prepared my Career Development Plan (CDP) to outline my plan to go to UCSB while working full time and get an advanced degree there. There was some skepticism, I am sure, within the Training section whether I would ever use these skills at DPR, but my CDP was approved, as was my request to have DPR help with funding the costs of going back to school.

Right around this time, El Capitan State Beach, about a twenty minute drive from the UC campus in Santa Barbara, was completing a major expansion and renovation of its campgrounds. Through this additional workload, the addition of supervisory staff had been justified and approved. I applied for a supervisory

43

ranger position, and along with Steve Michel, was selected. I remember clearly explaining in my interview how working at the Gaviota District fit in perfectly with my career AND educational goals.

Thank you so much for the book; I shall lose no time in reading it...

I dusted off my GRE exam scores from 1972, and to my surprise, the Geography Department at UCSB accepted them. I had been nervous about retaking the GRE exam, having been out of school for six years, so that was a relief. The Department Chair, Dave Simonett, looked at my quantitative score (far from my strong suit), told me that those scores do not go down, and accepted me into grad school. I did not mention that I was pretty sure that my scores were not going to go up, either.

Everything was looking good, or so I thought. I promoted to Gaviota in May of 1978 and even was assigned park housing at El Capitan. I spent the summer working a busy southern California beach park, and I was very excited about getting started in graduate school in the fall.

We found this great beach in Santa Barbara, and it was right next to the ocean...

During my first week of work, one of the park aids in the entrance station, Al Chistegrande or something like that, decided that either I was not a vindictive person, or that he no longer cared whether he had a job. I drove into the park one day, and Al told me there was an emergency in campsite 31 and I needed to go there right away. What Al did not tell me was that, through the process of the campground renovation, a little glitch in the campsite numbering system had occurred. The lower loop contained campsites 1 – 30, and the middle loop was composed of campsites 32 – 64. Yup, campsite 31 had been vaporized. It took me a few frantic trips through both loops before I realized that I had been had. I am sure Al got a kick out of seeing my vehicle race between the loops. I am also sure that Al must have enjoyed his next job, because, as it turns out, he was wrong about me not being vindictive...

One of the early explorers, looking for campsite 31

We want this to be effective – effective with a capital "A"…

The management at Gaviota was focused, oddly enough, on ensuring that no campsite ever had more than two vehicles in it at any given moment. Steve Michel and I tried like heck to get management to ease up on this, since it took an awful lot of time and effort and created lots of ill will. I knew I was spending too much time making "third vehicle" contacts when I found myself driving through the residential areas of nearby Goleta to make a bank drop or go to class, and I would start to pull over and make a contact whenever I saw more than two vehicles in someone's driveway. I would then have to remind myself that it was okay; it was a private driveway and the residents were allowed as many vehicles as the CCR's would allow. Maybe my retirement gig can be on the police force of a Homeowners' Association.

The Scottish word "sgiomlarieachd", which is even harder to pronounce than it is to spell, is defined as "the habit of dropping in at mealtimes."

Gaviota District had a weird assortment of rangers. Among them was Don, who lived in a park house at Refugio and, as far as anyone could tell, NEVER had to eat at home by himself. Don was handsome, charming, and, apparently, really quite hungry. Almost every time I saw Don, he was enjoying a meal at some camper's picnic table. He would wave to me when I drove by, but he never invited me to join him. After all, he explained, HE was not the hostess, and that it would be presumptuous and rude for him to invite me in. He would go on foot patrol before lunch or dinner and would strike up a conversation with some family that was cooking a meal that he deemed appealing. Many rangers would prioritize their visitor contacts based on, oh, say, evidence that something was amiss vis-à-vis park rules and regulations. I am pretty sure Don's priorities on contacting visitors were based more on his checklist of favorite camp meals and aromas. I don't know if he ever had to renege sometimes on meal offers if a better meal came along. How to choose? I mean, what dilemmas rangers sometimes face. Thank goodness for good training.

All the campers loved Don. I suspect that some of them loved him so much that he returned for dessert after hours. At his retirement party, a picnic table was set in the classic "Missing Man Formation" to honor Don's ability to scam free meals. His fondness for dessert was not mentioned.

My family camping at Refugio State Beach -- the only time we
ever went camping as a family. My sister-in-law Janie, I believe,
is looking for Ranger Don, to invite him to dinner.

Visitors who think the rangers are rude should see the Chief Ranger...

You know, I have heard retired rangers talk about having to walk
out of Bodie in the winter when their Snowcat broke down, and
being trapped in Big Basin by fallen trees, but nothing quite
compares with the rigors of working El Capitan in the late 70's –
having to endure the sound of the gentle surf and to watch the
activities on the beach and in the campsites for signs of
inappropriate behavior day after day, night after night. Sometimes
the daytime temperatures would soar into the high 70's, then
plunge that same night into the low 60's. Santa Barbara is about
as nice a city as you will find. The only drawback is that it does
not have professional sports teams. Now that I think about it, I am
not sure that San Diego has major league sports teams either.

I told her she shouldn't try that so soon, because you can't count your eggs 'til they come home to roost in the basket...

Next up was a character who called himself "El Greco". I will not relate what some of the campers called him. Remember, these rangers were hired before the days of background checks. Greco lived on a boat, but not one on the water like normal folks. Greco's boat was in storage at a nearby private campground, and he lived in the boat in the storage yard. I guess he liked having the salt spray of the ocean and the roar of the surf, well, nearby.

He was a dichotomy. Today, we might call him a trichotomy. One day he spent a couple of hours and hiked five miles or so along the railroad tracks that ran near the park to look for a missing child. Then the next day, he would spend a couple of hours ranting and raving to a park visitor about a minor infraction. Greco also made homemade elderberry wine. I learned right away (the hard way) that, should you choose to drink some of Greco's elderberry wine, you needed to be sitting on the toilet while drinking. Otherwise, before you could yell, "What the *Sambucus* is going on?" it would be too late. I petitioned to get elderberry on the endangered species list in order to end this madness, unsuccessfully.

For El Greco's annual performance review, I gave him a couple "Improvement Needed" ratings. These were in several categories, but most notably in wine-making. Anyway, Greco did not appreciate my ratings in the least, and told me that, after the summer was over, he was going to resign. He told me he would work through the summer, since it would be unfair to leave us short-handed in the summer. He accused me of thinking I was God, since I had the nerve to attempt to improve his performance. In his mind, I realized, his performance was perfect. Actually, had I been God, I would have persuaded him to resign before the summer. I reckoned it would not be worth the trouble to have him quacking around all summer as an unhappy and very lame duck.

That comment really shot the wind out of his saddles...

I think he started having second thoughts as the summer progressed, because he regularly kept informing me that he was serious about his decision to resign, and there would be nothing I could say that would change his mind. Then Greco would inform me that I WOULD be afforded one last chance to upgrade his performance review. Gee, how long do I get to decide on that offer? Right after Labor Day, Greco did resign. He then took the bold step of taking his boat out of storage and actually putting it in the ocean. His plan was to live on his boat and sail up and down the west coast. The only glitch in this plan was that he learned that his son had just graduated from voodoo school somewhere in the Caribbean, and that his son's final exam included, well, um, actually murdering his father. I don't know how the son did on the quantitative portion of the GRE to get into voodoo school, but I do know that Greco probably kept quiet about the exact details of his travel plans for a while.

As the fall of 1978 approached, I was excited about the prospect of going back to school. One of my tasks at work was to prepare the monthly schedule for permanent and season visitor services staff. Steve Michel, the other supervisor, was great about being flexible vis-à-vis the schedule. The fall catalogue came out, and I wrote up the schedule. Once the chief ranger saw the schedule, all hell broke loose.

That's just like the thief who yells fire in a crowded restaurant...

The only way to get the classes I needed was to split my days off. Classes were either offered on Mondays and Wednesdays or Tuesdays and Thursdays. So I had split my days off to take these classes, but of course I would not split Steve's days off. The Chief Ranger and the Area Manager called me in and told me I could not split my days off, and that I needed to take night classes. I showed them the catalogue, which showed them that UCSB at the time DID NOT OFFER night classes. My point was that my Career Development Plan and my Training Requests had been approved at the highest levels, and that I had been clear in my interview that my goal was to attend UCSB and get my MA in Geography. They were, however, intractable.

Fortunately for me the Regional Office was in Goleta, only a few miles down the road. I went down there to plead my case, and they approved my schedule on the spot. I was never too popular with the Gaviota managers after that.

Your work is both good and original. However, the good parts are not original, and the original parts are not good...

I was prepared for a tough two years of grad school and working full time. My plans were thwarted temporarily through a clever device at UCSB called "Multivariate Statistical Analysis". This class was not only required, but it was only taught once a year. In addition, it was unfathomable. To make matters worse, it was taught by TA's whose only English phrase was "Math universal language". Not only is that statement untrue, but I could not understand the TA's English when he would utter it. He uttered it frequently, most often when students complained that they did not understand his English.

Need I emphasize that the SECOND time I took this class I did much better, but that was probably due to my hiring a tutor. I clung to that tutor. Basically, I squeezed a two year program into a mere three years. Also, I really had the energy for two years, and for the third year I was running on what is left when the fumes are exhausted.

Sorry about the time; I got a late head start...

Another character at Gaviota was ranger Max, who lived in Oxnard, about forty-five minutes from El Capitan. Every day, Max would drive his Harley to work. That was really cool. The uncool thing was that Max was about ten minutes late to work, EVERY DAY. When I told him he needed to start getting to work on time (and "on time" meant ready to roll out in uniform and geared up, not just rolling in to the office,) Max responded that he lived in Oxnard – thirty miles away. Now you see, one of the jobs of a supervisor is to try to think of creative ways to solve problems wherein BOTH parties benefit; I have a phrase for this, and I call it a Win/Win situation. So with Max, I advised him to leave Oxnard at least fifteen minutes earlier every day. Those classes at Asilomar on how to be a good supervisor really gave me some brilliant ideas.

Sure there have been injuries and even some deaths in boxing, but none of them really that serious...

Then there was Ranger Bob. Ranger Bob was a rookie, but he already had advice for the Department on just about every facet of its operation and policies, and all of those facets were, in his opinion, ridiculous and outdated. His most vociferous complaint was about our defensive tactics training and policies. Bob was highly trained in martial arts -- an obscure branch called feng-shui, I believe -- and he liked to show off his black belt for all to see. Bob wanted all of the Department's peace officers to be trained as masters in feng-shui as well. One day at Asilomar, Bob and Ranger Mike made a little wager. Now Mike had been a fairly proficient boxer, so they decided to go a few rounds after class one day. They were so far ahead of their time; now people make millions in promoting Mixed Martial Arts. Anyway, they squared off, and Mike immediately leaned in, made a little head fake, and popped Bob in the nose, giving him a major nosebleed and knocking him on his ass. I never heard a word about the feng-shui proposal again, and Bob never got to be the DPR sensei.

Bob really should have been a highway patrolman, not a ranger. The three campgrounds of the Gaviota District (El Capitan, Refugio, and Gaviota State Beaches) are connected by US Highway 101, a freeway. We never had enough rangers to have one ranger assigned for any given shift to cover just one campground; at most we had two rangers on duty, so they usually had to cover more than one campground. So there was a lot of freeway driving for the rangers. And Ranger Bob, as the rookie, usually was on at night. Almost every night, Ranger Bob would make a vehicle stop on 101 for "suspected DUI". Then a few minutes later, Ranger Bob would let the driver go and head back on the highway. We would go round and round on this. My point was, sure, if there is a threat to public safety, you need to make a stop. But I do not remember him making one arrest. And how did so many drivers he pulled over pass the field sobriety test? Bob would swear the guy was weaving, changing speeds, on and on. I think he was just bored, and he finally went to a different enforcement agency. Feng-shui, last time I checked, had not been approved there either. Maybe Bob took up boxing.

One summer weekend, I sailed out to Santa Cruz Island with Ranger John. The other rangers asked if they could have a party at my house while I was gone. Gee, they never wanted a party when I WAS home. At least John and I had a great time.

Anyway, John and I sailed back the next morning; I returned home and lay down to rest before heading in for night shift. I smelled something funny, and it prevented me from resting well. I finally gave up and decided just to go into work early. I went to the closet in the bedroom to pull out my uniform, and I found the source of the smell. My uniform shirts and other dress shirts were covered in vomit! I went storming up to the ranger office and asked the assembled staff what in the tequila sunrise had happened. Ranger Bob got sheepish right away and said that he had had way too much to drink, and had decided to sleep in my bed rather than drive home. He remembers losing his cookies that night, but he said he must have mistaken my closet for the toilet. Hey, I am not THAT bad a housekeeper! He made the proper *mea culpas*, escorted me to my house, grabbed the shirts, and told me he would immediately have them all dry-cleaned and pressed. I thought that would be the end of it, but the cleaners had the practice of writing the last name of the client on the inside of the collar of every shirt they cleaned. So when I got my shirts back, nicely cleaned, they all had the name "Ranger Bob" indelibly inscribed thereon. For the next couple of years, every time I put on one of those shirts, I was reminded that yes, this shirt used to be covered in someone else's puke. When I moved back to San Diego, I finally donated all of them to a thrift store that specialized in clothing the married, horny nudists of Black's Beach.

In the late spring of 1981, it was time to leave the Gaviota District. It had been a fun, crazy, really busy three years. The Department, miraculously, coincided the timing of the Resource Ecologist exam with my proposed graduation from UCSB. In yet another miracle, they expanded the number of ecologist positions significantly, further enhancing my chances of getting a job in my newly chosen profession. Now if I could only nail down that pesky graduation.

I was burning the midnight oil from both ends...

UCSB offered its geography grad students the option of taking a comprehensive exam in lieu of completing a Master's thesis. Working full-time as a supervisor really made it difficult to perform the research necessary for a thesis, so I opted for the exam. I think I must have been the first to do so, because my advisor had to scramble to come up with how to conduct the exam. Finally we reached the solution; each of the three professors on my graduate committee would come up with three written questions for me. Then I was placed in a room for nine hours and was given the opportunity to write approximately one hour on each question. As you might guess, these were not true/false nor multiple choice questions. They actually made me think and required me to call upon my education, training, intelligence, judgment, reasoning, and so forth. That's right – I was in real trouble! And these were in the days of pen and paper; we did not have word processors.

I staggered out of the room nine hours later and handed my opus to my major advisor. This was on a Wednesday; graduation was to be on the Thursday eight days later. I did what every grad student living in a beach house would do, and scheduled a graduation party PRIOR to getting my results, on Friday night right after the exam.

Just because he's the landlord doesn't mean he owns the place...

The "Point House" at El Capitan was EPIC for parties. After all, I had learned from the experts – the lifeguards at Torrey Pines. And rather than a historic beautiful adobe home and office (Torrey Pines) the El Capitan house was really just an old shack, and it was difficult to find anything to damage on the house. Further, I was a single young guy, and I owned nothing that could be damaged (well, I did own a lava lamp and a Saturday Night Fever poster.) It was the only house around, so there were no neighboring residents, and it was out of sight and sound of the nearest public facility. Also, it was at least a hundred feet from the ocean, so anyone who passed out had a good chance of not being immediately swept away. It was, in a word, PERFECT. It was so perfect that the Department, shortly after I moved out, in a fit of enormous stupidity, burned it to the ground to get rid of it. I still think it might have made more sense just to install a toilet in the bedroom closet...

The "Point" House at El Capitan State Beach. My brother Mark, my dad, and me. Dad loved to practice his golf swing!

A picnic table and a beautiful woman -- all that are left at the site of the El Cap Point House. Hey, you can HAVE the picnic table!

Friday afternoon arrived, and I had not heard a word from my advisor. I guess that should have sent up warning signals, but I was busy getting ready for the party. Besides, I suspected my answers had been so brilliant that he probably got distracted while writing up his recommendation for me for the UCSB Ph.D. program.

Everyone lived through the party, and I recall that everyone was able to keep the closet separate from the toilet. Monday morning my advisor called and asked me to come in to the campus; we had things to discuss. Crap! I reckoned this discussion was NOT going to be his opportunity to plead with me to stick around to work on my doctorate after all.

The professor stood his ground and didn't run tail, but he did agree to do the poof reading...

He told me that I had passed eight of the nine questions, and that the one I failed was one of his questions. I don't recall the exact question, but I think it had something to do with geographic methods of dealing with arrogant, egomaniacal professors who try to ruin your future. I asked innocently what the problem with my answer was, because that was the one answer I felt the best about. He responded that he was looking for four points for me to cover, enumerated and described them, and said they were all missing. He said that failure of any one of the nine exam questions was failure of the entire exam, and since I was the first and only (and, quite possibly, the last) grad student who had ever chosen the exam route, he would have to consult with the Department Chair to see what recourse I might have. I could just picture ol' Dave Simonett looking up my old GRE scores once again and wondering how he could have been so wrong about me.

I asked to see my submittal, because I was pretty sure I had covered those four points. Unless someone had puked on my paper and obscured these points, I was not going down without a fight. Sure enough, my perusal revealed that I had indeed discussed those very four points. When I pointed this out to him, he reread my answers and became thoughtful, apparently thinking of how to save face in light of his major screw-up. He finally came up with the solution, which was to tell me I should have put them in a different order. He said that if I rewrote that one answer, put the points in HIS order, and got it back to him the same day, he would pass me.

He was suffering from a detached rectum...

So let's see; he screws up and I have to do the work. Oh well, it was worth it to me to have a relatively easy way to finish up at this point. Of course, today I would pull out my laptop, cut and paste, run the thumb drive over to a printer, and give him his new answer in about five minutes. But in 1981, I rewrote it all by hand and turned it in a few hours later. He passed me, and I graduated on time. I later heard that he was denied tenure and moved to a different university, but I do not claim any responsibility for that. I did go the extra step, however, and wrote a letter of recommendation for him to become the Superintendent of the Gaviota District. After all, I was outta there....

Every time I thought grad school was more than I could handle, I thought of a picture of my mother at her college graduation holding two LITTLE boys, and a picture of my grandmother at her graduation receiving her degree in paleontology. My Grandma's dad left the family, so her mom had to go to work. Grandma raised her three sisters while still in high school and then went on to get a B.S. in paleontology at Tulsa University.

It is time to step up the plate and lay all your cards on the table...

My interview for the resource ecologist position in San Diego was strange. Ron McCullough and Hal Terry were the interviewers, and it was held in Goleta. Ron never sat down once, and Hal never stood. I took the middle ground and squatted the whole time. Hal would ask a technical question, like, "If you were planning a prescribed burn in the pine understory on a western slope, what factors would you consider in your plan?" In short, a question that could take five minutes or so to answer and one that would reveal my thought process and grasp of the issues – I hated Hal's questions for those reasons. Then Ron would ask a question like, "Can you get along with other people?" I wasn't sure what he was driving at, but I answered in the affirmative. I left out the exception that I could not get along with the managers at Gaviota, but then I was not sure that they were actually people. Or he would ask, "If you recommended a position on an environmental issue, and the Regional Director decided to go in a different direction, could you support the Regional Director's decision? Or would you call up every stinkin' environmental group in the state to get them to write letters about it?" I wasn't sure what he was driving at, but I answered in the affirmative to the first part, and in the negative to the second part. I started to get the idea that perhaps, just perhaps, the other ecologist working at the Southern Region, James Polyesterino, may not be a team player.

BACK TO SAN DIEGO – RESOURCE ECOLOGIST

I was eventually hired to work at the Southern Region, in San Diego, which was my first choice of the locations available. I was young and intimidated about the prospect of working in the Regional Office in a job with a lot of responsibility; that intimidation disappeared the first morning. There were two stories to the building in Old Town San Diego; the lower level was for the grunts, while the bosses and their favorite staffers were upstairs. But for the first time in my life, I had my very own office.

Hemorrhoids are a real pain in the neck…

My boss, Hal Terry, was giving me a tour and introducing me to everyone, when Deputy Regional Director Ron McCullough bolted out of the restroom, clapping his hands and cackling with glee. Hal asked him what was up, and he said "Herb (Regional Director Herb Heinze) is taking a crap, the bathroom has no windows, and I just turned out the lights in there. Herb is swearing at me since he can't see a damned thing!" I felt like I was back in high school; I was more comfortable being in high school. A few days later I shut the lights off on Ron and I really laughed hard; he really laughed harder later as I cleared out my sole proprietor office and moved in to share office space with James, the other ecologist.

James and I were responsible for overseeing the resource management activities at the seventy-plus parks that composed the Southern Region. It was an overwhelming task, made more difficult by the fact that James had decided that the job was too big for one person and he was going to spend all his time at the beautiful (and nearby) Cuyamaca Rancho State Park. OK, let's just ignore the other sixty-nine parks, including some of the Department's finest units. So my job became to help with ALL the other parks, including the magnificent and huge (almost one thousand square miles) Anza-Borrego Desert State Park. The managers of these other parks had felt slighted, and rightly so.

For a minute, I really thought my ass was in a noose…

I guess the Regional managers wanted to start me off slowly, because my first assignment was to prepare a letter to be signed by Herb Heinze that outlined the Department's position on a City of San Diego proposal. Herb said to keep it under one page, which I did. He approved it, and then asked me to read it aloud into the testimony to be taken at a Coastal Commission hearing locally. I went to the meeting and signed up to speak. Then the Chair of the Coastal Commission called the meeting to order and said "We now invite Mr. Van Cleve to take us through this proposed project, and we ask him to keep his presentation under thirty minutes." Gee, I was really going to have to speak slowly to keep my presentation OVER thirty seconds. Just as I was about ready to puke on a lot of peoples' shirts due to stage fright, Jack Van Cleave, Director of Planning for the City of San Diego, rose and went to the lectern. He became my hero instantly, even though he spelled his name incorrectly and my letter was in opposition to the City's position.

You would not believe how often good things happen to bad people; somebody even wrote a book about it...

James left State Service a few months after my arrival. In the loving, supporting, nurturing style common to many managers of that era, Hal Terry then told me he was going to throw me into offices with some other losers in the hopes that they would quit too. Always happy to help where needed. Later, when Asilomar canvassed all employees to ask them to list their special skills, that was number one on my list. I think they were building a data base of employee skillsets. I am not sure that it was ever used.

With a ranger's hat and shovel and a pair of dungarees...

One activity undertaken by resource ecologists statewide was prescribed burning. Fire was seen a valuable resource management tool, and we took a lot of training in order to become certified as burn bosses by the state. In southern California, Cuyamaca Rancho State Park was seen as the primary park for fire to be applied to the forests, woodlands, and meadows. Unfortunately for the park, the progress of the burn program was not robust enough, and most of the park was hit very hard by the Cedar Fire of October, 2003.

We were burning at Cuyamaca in the fall of 1983 for several days, so several of us stayed at the No-tell Motel in nearby Julian. This little inn was, well, let us say, past its prime. But that was okay, since we did not have lot of money to spend on rooms. The first night, I just could not get comfortable in the bed. I am not saying the mattress and springs were too soft, but the left and right sides of the mattress were pretty much touching above me, and I could not find a comfortable way to sleep. I felt more like a hot dog than a quesadilla. Finally, I decided to put the mattress on the floor and try that. When I pulled the mattress of the bed, I saw that there was a door under the mattress – yes, a wooden door. Now I know that sometimes people put a sheet of plywood under a mattress in order to provide stiffness, and in this case the motel folks used a door instead of plywood. But you would think they would have had the brains to TAKE THE DOORKNOB OFF! I am not exactly the princess and the pea, but that was ranunculus!

The problem is we have too many Indians and not enough chickens…

Ron McCullough, "Mac", was a character. He was a great Regional Director, as were Herb Heinze and Ken Jones. I thought Ken was the last great Southern Region Director. Oh yeah…he WAS the LAST Southern Region Director, because the region concept got eliminated in the early 90's. Mac would get really mad, and he would not hide his anger. Then a few minutes later he would calm down, and everything would be back to normal. Psychologists say this is healthy; it certainly was NOT healthy for me…

When Mac was still the Deputy Regional Director and Herb the Regional Director, I put in a package to upgrade the associate resource ecologist position to the senior level. As the importance of the resource management function in parks grew, we were able to add staff to assist with implementing the program. There was a large pool of talented biologists anxious to do resource work. As we added staff, our ability to protect the resources in the field was expanded tremendously. It was this growth in staff and program size that gave us regional ecologists the idea that we should place our resource programs on a par with Visitor Services and Technical Services.

Jim Dice watching Karen Miner do all the work on vegetation plots

In a bureaucracy, you need to have a ton of justification, which I did (the other three regions were pursuing the same course of action, which also helped). I also had a good candidate in mind, since James Polyesterino had already left. Anyway, I had not heard anything on the progress of the "package" for months, and one day I ran into Herb Heinze in the elevator and asked him if he knew what was going on with my promotion package. He said he would look into it.

And then the fan really hit the roof...

The next thing I knew, Mac was in my office screaming at me never to go behind his back again. So it was okay for Mac to sit on my package without acting on it for six months, but I guess it was not okay to ask the boss about it. But the real point is that Mac stormed out of my office while I considered my DEMOTIONAL opportunities. I called Personnel to see if they had a form I could use to plan out the death spiral my career was now entering. Less than ten minutes later, Mac was back in my office asking me what I thought the Padres' chances were this year. For once, I avoided making any wisecracks or stupid comments.

Don't judge a man until you've walked a mile in an open can of worms...

The staff at the Region shared vehicles, which made sense. I eventually became head of the "resource" section at the Region, on a par (on paper at least) with the more traditional Visitor Services Section and the Technical Services Section. Each section had a primary vehicle or two, but once in a while you had to "borrow" a vehicle from another section. The unwritten rule was that you had better leave the vehicle clean and gassed up at the end of your trip, or you might not get permission to use it the next time. So one day I needed to borrow the Chrysler Concorde from Visitor Services. Now the Concorde was probably the ugliest, most uncomfortable, gutless car of its day. I can imagine the fleet buyers at General Services rubbing their hands in glee as they imagined thousands of hapless, unsuspecting state employees trying to get somewhere in the Chrysler Concorde (R.I.P.). I think it lost races to the Pinto and the Maverick.

Anyway, this certain Friday, I took the car up to Cuyamaca Rancho State Park for a meeting. On the way back to the office, after a sumptuous repast at the local "Squat and Gobble," I stopped at the Manzanita Ranch in Wynola; I bought a quart of raw apple cider there and put it on the floor of the rear seat. I AM POSITIVE that I did not stop between Wynola and the Region office, but when I got back there the bottle of cider had disappeared. I searched the back seat, under the seats, in my shirt pockets, in the trunk...everywhere. But I could not find my cider. I finally gave up (it was late on a Friday afternoon), locked up the car in the outdoor parking lot, and went home for the weekend.

That road had a lot of hiccups...

I was back at work on Monday, when Paul, my peer in the Visitor Services section, came storming into my office asking what I had done to "his" car. I had no idea what he was talking about, so he took me out to the parking lot, where all the doors on the car were wide open, and you could smell the car from a hundred feet away. That darned bottle of raw cider had rolled under the seat, and I guess I must have run over someone on the drive back to the office, for the bottle jumped up with all its might and wedged itself in the seat springs. So when I had looked under the seat, the bottle was up in the springs hiding from me. I swear if you tried to make this happen, you would be unsuccessful in one thousand attempts. Then, over the hot weekend, the cider kind of, well, fermented, blew the lid off, and spewed hard cider all over the floor of the Concorde. It really did stink. I offered to do anything to make this right. Paul suggested we switch cars permanently. Well, anything but THAT. He was NOT getting my AMC Pacer! Of course, had I totaled the Concorde, the Visitor Services guys would have thanked me, because they could have replaced the Concorde with something spiffy, like, say, a Ford Courier. Those darned guys were mad at me for a year. Paul never came into my office to ask me how I thought the Padres would do that year. But you see, that is unhealthy – to get mad and STAY mad. I am still pissed off about his anger...

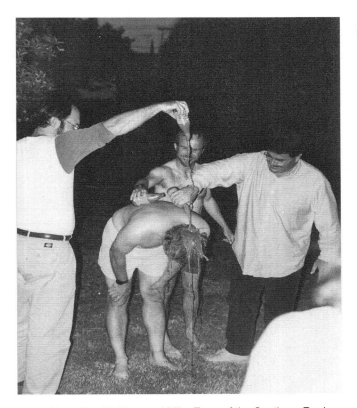

Jim Dice, Clay Phillips, and Mike Tope of the Southern Region waterboarding me for stinking up the Chrysler Concorde. For some reason, Chocolate YooHoo Soda was the torture instrument of choice. I manned up and finally confessed that James did it.

He took to it like a fish out of water...

I was fortunate to be trained as a state SCUBA diver. Even better were the job duties. A lot of State Parks divers are trained to do searches for bodies in the numerous reservoirs operated by the Department. What a job -- about a foot of visibility, looking for a dead person, mostly by feel rather than by sight. My dive partner, Bill Tippets, and I were assigned the job of doing underwater scientific research and interpretive planning – a much nicer assignment. The training was at Scripps Institute in La Jolla and was conducted by Divemaster Jim Stewart – truly a diving legend, and reportedly a contemporary of Jacques Cousteau.

First, though, I had to pass the swim test. I had practiced hard for the swim test, which was held in the UC San Diego fifty meter indoor pool. One thing I noticed right away was that the other three guys in the SCUBA class were lifeguards, say, about twenty-five years old on average. That's right – they were at the height of their physical prowess and veterans of the competitive swimming and water polo teams in their respective high schools, colleges, and probably even Olympic teams. I, on the other hand, was in my mid-thirties and had begun to display hints of endomorphism, even at that tender age.

We had to swim a thousand meters, and it was timed. After about four of the required twenty laps, I noticed, through my keen powers of observation, that none of the three lifeguards appeared to be still in the pool. Now it was impossible that they had finished already; then I looked down and these darned guys were dolphin kicking every lap on the bottom of the pool. And they were WAY ahead of me! They were doing fifty meter laps underwater on one breath, while Jim Stewart probably thought I was doing an imitation of an alligator wrestler on the surface of the pool. Jim came over and said the sweetest words a SCUBA student ever heard; "You are doing fine; don't worry about those assholes."

There were a couple of interesting moments during the two week training. On the first Monday morning, Jim Stewart started the course. Jim wore a short sleeved shirt, and his elbow and arm were absolutely mangled and did grab your attention. After a while, Fred, one of the students, raised his hand and asked Jim what had happened to his arm. I think Fred may still have been in oxygen deficit from doing too many underwater laps without a breath. Jim glared at the student, and growled, "That's Wednesday's lecture!" It turns out Jim had been attacked by a grey reef shark in the South Pacific, and he subsequently wrote a monograph on the pre-attack behavior of this shark species. I hope I never get to write a paper on the pre-attack behavior of ANY predator. Or peri- or post-attack behavior, for that matter.

There is enough water here to sink a fish...

One night we were scheduled to do a night dive. This was in December, and even in San Diego the water is cold. But with proper dive equipment, the cold was not a factor. December is also a big month for the migration of gray whales in the waters off San Diego. Sure enough, we four students were on our night dive when a whale ambled by. I don't know how big it really was, but it looked HUGE to us. Without a word or any pre-arranged diver signal, we all immediately went to the surface. We were not sure why we surfaced; it was instinctive, I guess.

That fish won't hunt...

The funniest drill was the night dive that tested our navigation skills. We had cool Diver Joe SCUBA compasses on our wrists, and we were given the task of swimming a large triangular course that, if we kept to our headings, would bring us right back to our starting point – the Scripps Pier. So Jim Stewart stood at the end of the pier, and he could see our headlamps as we swam the nav course. Even more helpful for navigation than the compasses was the light that was located right at the end of the pier where Jim stood. I think he liked to stand under the light and admire his shark bite scar. Fortunately, the light was about eight million watts. So on my final leg of the triangle, I would look at my compass, convinced that I had done all my calculations correctly and was on a course that would bring me right to the end of the pier. Then I would look up and double check the location of the pier light, and would correct my course gently, oh, by about twenty degrees or so. Jim complimented us all on our perfect navigation skills when we arrived EXACTLY at the end of the pier. Actually, I think on day one Jim saw that we all were very comfortable in the water (all four of us were already advanced open water divers), so he was able to have fun along with us. He accompanied us on a few training dives and used about half the air we did.

There is a lot of steak on the line here...

My favorite project ever as an ecologist was the cattle removal project at Anza-Borrego. One of my jobs as the regional ecologist was to parcel out resource management funds to the parks of the region. You can probably imagine the drill: I would call for proposals for projects for the year, parks would respond, I would choose the most appropriate projects, the parks would complete the projects. At least, that is how it was supposed to work. We had a fiscal year of July 1 – June 30, and usually a lot of the recipients would call around April and say they would not be able to complete their projects, and the funds would have to revert (go bye-bye for good). The one exception was Anza-Borrego, and the main reason for their success was that all their projects would be managed by Mark Jorgensen. I discovered that if I gave Mark $5,000, he would complete a $20,000 project, since he would go out and get funds from other sources. Plus he would see the project through to its completion. Guess who started getting the nod when project proposals were a close call in terms of funding.

If you let that sort of thing go on, your bread and butter will be cut right out from under your feet...

So in 1987, Mark proposed that all the feral cattle be removed from the park, due to the risk that cattle posed to the endangered (and native) bighorn sheep. Mark had originally persuaded a State Senator to introduce a bill that permitted, on a one-time basis, cattle to be shot in the park. The California Cattlemen's Association got that bill killed in about 1.6 seconds. Of course, that proposed action would have saved a ton of money.

They'll never buy the cow if they already get their eggs for free...

So the next idea was to hire aerial teams that would capture and remove the cattle alive. This would be done through helicopters that netted the cattle from the air. A ground team would blindfold and hobble each animal, and then it would be attached in the net to the bottom of the helicopter and flown out to a holding pen. From there, the cattle would be transported to Brawley for live auction. Of course, the Anza-Borrego cattle were skinny, having thrived on desert vegetation -- not corn, lush grass, or other feed. So they were ignored at auction, and had to be destroyed anyway. The park eventually spent about $500.00/cow, rather than the small fraction of that it would have cost had hunting been allowed; and every animal wound up dead eventually anyway.

Getting ready to hook a captured cow to the
helicopter for a nice flight back to camp.

We had to get all our ducks on the same page...

I approved the funding for the project, and we got underway.
Contractors were hired, environmental documents (CEQA) were
finalized, all the appropriate agencies were notified, and the
California Cattlemen's Association was satisfied.

It looks like all the cows have come home to roost...

It all started off quickly. The first fifty cattle never knew what hit
them. They were captured and flown back to the Horse Camp
corrals, and hauled off to Brawley. Then it took a lot longer for the
next fifty. They were more wary, more scattered, more hidden.
They were better at hiding than the maintenance staff at the
Gaviota District. Our staff would take turns at various jobs. One
option was to be one of the "cowboys" in the helicopter. After the
trained netgunner had captured a cow alive in his capture net, we
cowboys would alight from the helo, and subdue it. (I wonder if
real cowboys use words like "alight", "eschew", and "subdue.")
We would transfer it into a haul net, which was much sturdier.
Then the helo would return, we would hook the haul net to the
bottom of the bird, and off they went. One of the wranglers said

that he never thought that, in his lifetime, he would see a cow fly, but that he was wrong. The professional wranglers were from New Zealand. These guys would wear short shorts, eschew gloves and other protective gear, and were linear in their approach to catching cattle. Not linear thinkers; just linear. Whereas I would run from the helo to the captured bovine in a route that, well, tried to avoid cholla, barrel cactus, ocotillo, rattlesnakes, mesquite, etc., the Kiwis would go in a straight line and just wind up bloody as hell. They never complained. I had a couple of "owies" every day. But I "cowboyed up" and never filed a workers' comp claim. In fact, we were proud of the fact that through this entire, pretty dangerous project, no workers' comp claims were filed (and we only killed three staff.)

Mark Jorgensen and I prepare to transfer a
small bull from a capture net to a haul net.

Another job was to wait at the Horse Camp and help with the cattle when they arrived aerially. The helo would lower them gently into the corral, we would gently remove the blindfold and hobbles, gently remove the haul net, then RUN LIKE HELL for the fences of the corral and vault over. Some of the large bulls were sumbitches, and angry ones at that.

But there was a lot of down time. We talked Wallace, one of the wranglers, into teaching us greenhorns how to "throw rope", or throw a lasso around the neck of a live animal. Of course, we practiced on hay bales, fence posts, and the ever shifty and elusive Frank Padilla. I remember that Wallace advised me to think of throwing rope as "placing a teacup on the shelf". I don't remember putting too many teacups away successfully in my life, but I got the concept. After all, we cowboys drink strong coffee while we filter the grounds through our teeth…

Stay clear of her; she has a real spur under her saddle…

One day, the inmates from La Cima work camp were at the Horse Camp chopping wood, stringing barbed wire, practicing safe cracking, or whatever "make work" project their crew boss could come up with. Oh yeah, La Cima was an all-female work camp at the time.

That's grabbing the bull by the horns of a dilemma…

It just so happened that the helo brought into the corral a small, 500 pound young bull. At least I called him a bull. Since he was small, I got the bright idea that I should practice my rope throwin' (g's are always silent in this type of work) on a real, live, bull. After all, I lived not too far from the Tijuana bull ring, I had seen the running of the Pamplona bulls on TV, and I had read a bunch of Hemingway. In other words, I was ready. The female inmates got word that I was going to go mano a toro with this beast, and they jumped up on the rails of the corral and yelled what I took to be, um, encouragement. I was never quite sure if they were rooting for the bull or me.

I must not have been the sharpest marble in the drawer…

I was encouraged by the fact that my success rate on roping bales of hay was less than fifty percent, and this bullito was running around the corral like crazy. But sure enough, my first "teacup" landed right around his neck, and I turned to the ladies, bowed, and smiled. Of course, I had not planned for what happened next. Unlike hay bales, the bull kept moving, and, at five hundred

71

pounds, was a LOT more than I could handle. I must have looked like I was in a cartoon – arms stretched out, heels dug in, body at about a forty-five degree angle, and just flat-ass being yanked around the corral. Frank Padilla sensed my predicament, which I believe was approaching Code Red, and, oh, about eight – ten minutes later, in a moment of horrible judgment, jumped in to help. Unfortunately, he grabbed the same end of the rope that I had, and now we were both in cartoon mode. The inmates were going crazy, and I could hear them roaring "You Go, Cowboy!" above all else. Finally, Mark Jorgensen had a bright idea. After another ten minutes or so, he jumped into the corral, ran up to the bull, and chest butted it. All four of us went sprawling in the dust. I heard later that several of the La Cima inmates re-enlisted that day.

They sure got a great milk cow when they crossed a Holstein with a Burma bull…

Then it REALLY slowed down. We had estimated the feral cattle population at eighty. Of those eighty, we only captured 142 cattle. Hey, I never said I was a GOOD ecologist. But the last forty-two were ornery and hard to find. Of all the captured cattle, only three or four had ear tags or brands. So we had been dealing with a population that had been born in and had lived their entire lives in the park. I did feel a little better when I heard that twenty years later, The Nature Conservancy only captured 5200 of the 500 feral pigs it estimated were living on Santa Cruz Island.

She used enough Scotch tape to feed a third world country…

We eventually got all the cattle out of the park. That week, the San Diego TV news did a spot on the project. Their story lasted twenty seconds and contained eight factual errors. I don't know if I can talk fast enough to commit an error in fact every 2.5 seconds, but this reporter could. Twenty-five years later, I still have not heard one report of any cattle in the park. Total success, mostly due to Mark's perseverance and hard work.

Necessity is the mother of strange bedfellows…

Mark also was able to justify the acquisition of an airplane for Anza-Borrego Desert State Park. It made sense – a park of almost one thousand square miles with extreme weather conditions and rugged topography. So the request was finally approved, the funds were allocated, and the aircraft was purchased. However, as often happens with bureaucracies, the personnel side was not ready at the same time as the equipment purchase side. So the manufacturer delivered the aircraft, but there was no pilot yet on staff to fly the darn thing. And we just knew that some bureaucrat in Sacramento would figure out that we had a piece of equipment that was not being used and yank it back, after all that work to obtain it in the first place. So a couple of licensed pilots – District Superintendent Jim Hendrix and I – were trained and approved to fly the plane until Ranger/Pilot Gene Hammock was hired. The plane purchased was a Christen Husky, which greatly resembled the Piper Super Cub – high wing, big motor, and fabric wings – a light but powerful plane. The whole idea was to have an aircraft that could fly slowly and close to the ground, but had the power to climb out of bad situations. It was to be used for search and rescue as well as law enforcement situations, both of which demanded that it be low and slow.

I had a blast flying that plane, but it was a workhorse and not built for comfort. I was pretty beat after four - five hours in the plane, so I greatly appreciated and admired the REAL pilots' ability to put in seven - eight hour days in that plane. Since it had a very low stall speed (about forty-five knots), one of my goals was to find a strong headwind and see if I could fly the plane backwards, relative to the ground. I never could quite do it, but Gene Hammock told me later that he had about a fifty-five knot headwind one day, flew right into it, and saw the shadow of the plane moving slowly, ever so slowly, backwards on the ground. One of my "bucket list" goals was fulfilled when I flew the plane for my last time, and walked away safely. Imagine – my bucket list includes things for me to STOP doing. As the saying goes, a mid-air collision can ruin your whole day, and it was time for me to turn over flying to others. I think part of my decision to quit flying was spurred by seeing F-14's flying SIDEWAYS several times through Split Mountain -- part of my aerial patrol territory. The Husky would have been like a bug splat on their windshield.

We are being told they will call off the search for victims in one hour and fifteen minutes, Pacific Daylight Time...

Gene Hammock had the best flying story ever. In the summer, the plane fills a great mission by looking for people in trouble due to the extreme heat. With temperatures well over a hundred degrees every day, heat events can turn into heat fatalities easily. Every ranger at Anza-Borrego has tales to tell about heat-related emergencies – sometimes about when they personally get into thermal trouble. One hot summer day Gene was flying over Split Mountain, when he espied a vehicle with the hood propped up and the tracks of three people heading down the canyon. Not good. He flew in their direction and soon found them attempting to hike out in the heat. Not smart. The plane had a public address system, so Gene circled the three adults (one man and two women) and asked "Is everything OK?" All three people waved, and Gene realized he had asked the question in a way that did not provide a good way to respond. Did the wave mean everything was fine or not? So he circled back around, and this time he said, "If you need help, wave an article of clothing over your head." Gene reported that the two women both removed their shirts and waved them vigorously over their heads, and that one of the women was wearing a bra! Gene considered telling them that if they needed help right away, to remove their pants and do the hokey-pokey, but discretion took over at that point.

The pilot told them that a ranger would be there soon, and he called in to report the incident and request immediate ranger assistance on the ground. Amazingly, Ranger Manfred Knaak got the call and was the first to respond. Manfred is a native of Germany and is fluent, and the group in trouble was from Austria. Their letter of thanks expressed their amazement that the park was prescient enough to send out its German-speaking ranger.

He really threw a monkey into THAT wrench...

For some time, we knew that at some point we would need to take on the task of removing off-highway vehicles from Anza-Borrego; this, we knew, was going to be very, very difficult. It was made even tougher by the fact that the Director of the Department at that time initially opposed the proposal. But park staff like Mark Jorgensen, Joe von Hermann, and Jim "Purple Haze" Hendrix had the courage to see it through. There needed to be a lot of people pulling hard in the same direction at the same time, and the timing needed to be just right.

In order to be able to catch transgressors on dirt bikes, we were
trained how to ride motorcycles off-highway at Anza-Borrego. The
flaw in this logic was that WE ACTUALLY CARED
if we lived or died, apparently in contrast to the young men and
women we were trying to apprehend. (c.1973)

One of the key people to get on board was the Regional Director,
Ron McCullough. So my job at the region was to get Mac to
support the proposal and then have him sell it up the channels.
Fortunately, Mac was not afraid of a fight if it was for the right
cause, and he was a great believer in Park ideals.

Mac wanted to build support throughout the Department, and he
knew that if there were full support from the Department's leaders,
this would influence the Director. So he arranged a field trip to
Anza-Borrego that included all the Division Chiefs, Regional
Directors, Director's staff, and other key staff. Once they saw the
actual damage that was occurring in the field, there was really no
dissent – there was full consensus that the off road vehicles had
to leave the park. I believe that what tilted the decision in our
favor was the fact that the spacious Ocotillo Wells State Vehicular
Recreation Area was right next to Anza-Borrego Desert State

Park, and offered tens of thousands of acres of legal riding areas. Decision makers did not have to eliminate a popular activity; they merely had to move it next door to a legally sanctioned off-road area.

Being shorthanded really rakes havoc...

The best moment of the field trip was when we went out to Fish Creek. Mark Jorgensen was leading the field trip, and we met up with Ranger Tim Davis. He hiked all of us (about twenty-five people) over a little rise, and there we saw a bunch of "donuts" and other tracks where a couple of motorcycles had totally torn up this little patch of the park. Tim said, "It probably only took about fifteen minutes or so for these guys to tear this up, but it will take me eight hours or so to rake out their tracks." Chief Deputy Director Les McCargo, a career park veteran, looked at Mark and said, "Well, Mark, if you had been thinking, you would have brought twenty five rakes, and we could all have pitched in and raked out these tracks in fifteen minutes." Mark did not skip a beat, and responded, "Well, Les, I know you would be good at that job, since you have been raking out your own tracks for your whole career!" There was moment of stunned silence while everyone tried to stifle their laughter and look for a place to hide (I personally contemplated throwing up on my OWN shirt sleeve), then Les totally cracked up. Unbeknownst to most of us, Mark and Les were good friends and had recently travelled together on state business. Whewwwww....

It's time to split the baby with the bathwater...

It did take a while, but we did prevail. I had really good friends -- Parks people for whom I had a lot of respect -- call me during the process and tell me that we were nuts, and that we should come up with a compromise that the Director could support. But I was convinced that the park staff had could up with a good plan, and it was important to shoot for the right outcome.

I thought that I was doing a pretty good job as an ecologist. After a few years, Regional Director Herb Heinze retired, and Deputy Regional Director Ron McCullough was hired to replace Herb. I was careful not to take a crap in any windowless bathroom while

Ron was around. Or if I did, I was sure to carry a flashlight or headlamp with me.

The mid-80's at the Southern Region. I cannot remember why I received the flowers.

It's time to turn over a clean slate...

I got some insight into Ron's assessment of my career path one day, when he suggested that we take a trip together to Red Rock Canyon State Park, in the Mojave Desert. We drove up to Lancaster and got a couple of rooms. Ron was a huge sports fan, an interest we shared. So Ron suggested we just find a sports bar, have a couple of beers, munch on the snacks at happy hour, and call that dinner while we watched a ball game. Sounded good to me. Except that after the beers and the "dinner", Ron told me he was still hungry. And, since he was the Regional Director, that meant we were now going to dinner. Except that when we got to the restaurant, Ron suggested we have a couple of drinks before dinner. In my mind, these were actually after dinner drinks, but clearly I was not thinking clearly. So we had a couple of cocktails, and then sat down to a full dinner. I ordered ice water to drink. Ron next ordered a bottle of wine; after all, how can you eat

77

dinner without wine? I was totally toasted by then and did not touch the wine, but the bottle was empty at the end of dinner. I do not remember how it got emptied. All my energy by then was put into hoping that we were not going out at that point for a few after-dinner drinks. By now, I was so well "lit" that I did not even bother taking a light with me to the restroom.

During dinner, Ron started asking me why, um, "I was wasting my time on this stupid resource ecologist B.S." Up until that point, I thought I was in an important, well-respected job. Actually, it became clear (not sure how anything became CLEARER at that point) that Ron was actually coaching me vis-à-vis my career. It is probably a technique no longer taught in "Coaching and Mentoring" books, but it was effective, nevertheless.

It sounded like chalk screeching on a blackboard...

The next day, as we were driving to Red Rock State Park, Ron returned to the topic, since he probably figured that I did not remember much of our previous discussion. He was not trying to demean my work or my profession; on the contrary, he was trying to coax me to return to the field by applying for Superintendent positions. I had been a resource ecologist for eight years (after nine as a ranger), and I figured I was probably about halfway through my career with State Parks. And clearly, superintendents had the most awesome job in the Department, especially if you were far away from Sacramento and the Regional Office. So I applied for the next Superintendent III exam. My good fortune continued when I went to my interview to get on the list, and Ron was on the panel, sitting there smiling.

I could hear the handwriting on the wall...

I did well on the exam, so I started the age-old practice of trying to match up the names at the top of the list with the current and expected vacancies at that level. The jungle drums start beating, and you start to get a sense for how the first round of promotions from the list will fall into place.

ANZA-BORREGO and the COLORADO DESERT DISTRICT

In addition to working well with the staff of Anza-Borrego, I was also impressed with their park ethos and their sense of purpose. Even more importantly, the District Superintendent there, Jim Hendrix, told me that he was getting close to retiring. I set my sights on Anza-Borrego to land as a Superintendent III.

Anza-Borrego is one of the most unusual parks in the State Parks System. To begin with, it is huge! For a while, we could say that it composes half of the acreage of California's State Park System. While that is no longer true, it is well over forty-five percent. And it is magnificent. From just over sea level, the mountains in the park rise to over 6,000'. The scenic, cultural, and natural resources are wonderful; then add in a unique paleontological resource. So for a resource guy like me, it was the place I wanted to be.

Snow in Anza-Borrego Desert State Park,
and the world's cutest three-year-old. (c. 1995)

Not until frozen pigs fly in hell...

Of course, there are drawbacks as well. It is in the Sonoran Desert, and the summers are brutal. The park headquarters are in Borrego Springs, a small remote town. So even if a park professional were attracted to working there, it was often difficult for their spouse to find meaningful work in town. One prospective employee came to Borrego Springs for the first time to interview for a vacancy. He stopped at Crawford overlook on Montezuma Grade to get a perspective on the town and the Park, and his wife almost talked him into turning around right then. She called the view "a pile of rubble". But it is very nice rubble. He wound up taking the job, but his wife was a registered nurse, and she could never find professional work as an RN. They left after two years.

We should continue to ride the horse that brings in the gravy...

And the management issues were enormous and challenging. For one, the town is surrounded by the park. So any talk of "entrance fees" means something different in Borrego. Establishing an entrance fee might mean that if someone could not pay it, we might have to keep them out of the park and not allow them to get to their home in Borrego Springs. Maybe for some that would be a blessing. Or, if they were in Borrego and trying to get to San Diego or Palm Springs, and they were broke, we might have to keep them in the park and provide housing and shelter. Just kidding, but it made for interesting discussions. The town is the donut hole and the park is the donut. Typically, the center of a park is the most protected, since it is the farthest from civilization, but at Anza-Borrego, there was a town in the middle of the park.

Another example of ham-fisted salami slicing by those damn bean counters...

Anza-Borrego has also always been severely underfunded. But it is worth it to be able to work on important, big issues. I used to tell Regional Director Ken Jones that Anza-Borrego was forty-five percent of the Department's land base, had sixty percent of its big issues, and operated on just three percent of the Department's budget. Ken would respond that since I had arrived at Anza-Borrego, it also represented ninety percent of the Department's whining. It was hard to one-up Mr. KB Jones.

It is important to get into the backcountry of the parks occasionally and talk about park philosophy with those who are able to look towards the future. Mark Jorgensen, Dick Troy, Ronie Clark, Ted Jackson, and me on Villager Peak in the Santa Rosa Mountains.

I'd walk a mile in a camel's shoes to pass through the eye of a needle...

As mentioned previously, there is an official off-road park adjacent to Anza-Borrego. Ocotillo Wells State Vehicular Recreation Area (SVRA) was created in the 70's to help satisfy the demand of the rapidly growing off-road recreation community. This made sense in a lot of ways, since you had a viable alternative to people riding "green sticker" vehicles in the park. For many years, however, as this activity was growing, park staff allowed green sticker vehicles access to the park's five hundred or so miles of dirt roads. But eventually, staff and others started to realize that the off road use and the enjoyment of the park were becoming incompatible, and it may be necessary to remove the off-highway vehicles from park

81

areas and make them use the SVRA instead. Of course, it usually is easier to prevent an activity that has never occurred in a place than to eliminate that use once it has become established. Further, the motorcycles and dune buggies would use the businesses in Borrego Springs to buy gasoline, ice, groceries, meals, etc., so the issue had ramifications for the local economy.

This larger issue is faced by many park managers – "gateway" communities grow up next to parks to provide services the park cannot or does not provide, such as hotels, restaurants, recreational equipment sales and rentals, and other amenities. Then the leaders of those communities often oppose park policies or practices that favor the park over the local businesses. One good example was the 1988 wildfires in Yellowstone National Park. The business owners of West Yellowstone complained to their elected officials that the park's policy on not fully suppressing the fire was hurting them economically. Another example there would be the park's desire to restrict snowmobiling in the park, and again the business community fought the decision politically.

You can dish it out but you cannot take it with you...

Also, the desert is viewed differently by a lot of people. For a long time, the desert was considered a wasteland, and a region you tried to traverse as quickly as possible to get to your real destination. The desert is thought of as the place where you can place prisons, transmission lines, landfills, nuclear waste storage, and other facilities with little damage. Rather than have the places that create the need for infrastructure deal with those issues, society would rather just dump those problems in the desert.

Now the issue is renewable energy. We all understand the need and the desire to develop alternative sources of energy. But there should be strong consideration given to placing those facilities and the means of getting energy to the market in the least impactful locations possible. Facilities like the Sunrise Powerlink and Ocotillo Express were rushed through without adequate consideration of their impacts on the desert resources. Okay, enough of the soapbox, but it is a valid point.

The most rewarding feedback I would get on Anza-Borrego, and I got it often, was from managers in the National Park Service. Invariably, the superintendents of places like Mojave, Death Valley, and Joshua Tree National Parks would shake their heads when discussing Anza-Borrego Desert State Park and comment that they wished it were a National Park. Enough said.

Will you be hiring the new superintendent in-house or out-house...

Jim Hendrix did retire in 1989, and I was interviewed for the Anza-Borrego job by Ken Jones, the new regional director for southern California. Again, fortune smiled on me, because there were only two candidates, including me, for the position of superintendent. And the other candidate called me up to assure me that he did not want the Borrego job; the superintendent position he wanted was coming up in a month or two, and he wanted the drill of finding out what Ken Jones' interviews were like. Ken called me soon after the interviews to let me know the great news that I was headed to Anza-Borrego. I figured this assignment would be my career capstone, and I moved to Borrego Springs in August, 1989.

They wanted to see me go to town like a house of fire...

I think that some of my colleagues in the Resource Management Division in Sacramento thought I was "selling out" by going back to the field. I believed then, and even more so now, that District Superintendent is one of the most influential and important positions in the Department. At the Colorado Desert District, I was told that the superintendent is the Department's ambassador in that part of the state. I was empowered to meet with elected officials, the media, the big dogs of other federal, state, and local agencies, and to make decisions on behalf of the Department. Of course, my Division Chief would want to be kept informed on important issues. In part because of lean staffing, and in part due to the fact that the district is a long way from Headquarters, the district superintendent is given a long leash (or is it a noose?) At my retirement party, Dick Troy and Steve Treanor (retired bosses) sang a duet about how they totally ignored me at the Colorado Desert District. I think it was a compliment. I am not saying they TOTALLY ignored me, but at the retirement party my wife had to remind me who they were.

83

Steve Treanor and Dick Troy singing Willie Nelson's "You Were Always On My Mind" at my retirement party, January 2004.

I wanted to come out of the chute on the right foot...

I also thought that, although it could be great for my career, there was risk as well. If I stayed in San Diego or closer to civilization, I could make better connections as a Superintendent and be more influential. I could not have been more wrong. Since Anza-Borrego was such a great park, lots of important people would come there. Also, in town was a magnificent resort – La Casa del Zorro – where corporate retreats were common and where influential partners could stay in comfort. Once these people were in town, they often would want to talk to the park superintendent at some point. I got to meet some very key people – people who were tremendously helpful to me in my career and my life. I also met the love of my life there – my delightful and adorable wife, Mary.

Mary is one of those women comfortable camping on the beach, singing on stage, or putting on the charm at a black tie dinner.

I wanted to be sure not to build ourselves a bag of worms...

When you talk about Anza-Borrego with other park veterans, you get a sense for the importance of the place. Those who worked there in some capacity, almost unanimously, state that it was the best assignment of their career. Others say they really wish they could have worked there for a while, but their spouse could not have handled it. Oddly, although Borrego Springs is a retirement town, not too many park retirees settle there. Some of those that do have two retirement residences – one for the summer and one for the winter. It was, without question, the greatest assignment of my career.

You can't change a book by its cover...

Every year in town there is held what is known as the Peg Leg Liars' Contest. It is held one evening with a big campfire and a whole bunch of alcohol, and participants get up and tell a whopper about the mythical Peg Leg and his lost cache of gold. When I got to town, the local deputy sheriff was the chief judge of the contest. I approached him one day and told him that I wanted to enter the contest. He immediately told me I could not enter, since it was for amateurs only! He laughingly told me that I was a cop, and that not only did I work for the state, but I was a manager for the state, and those three factors automatically provided me with PROFESSIONAL liar status. What a hoot he was!

I guess parks have always had budget issues. When I arrived at the park in 1989, the office was a joke. There was a security system, and the passcode was written on a piece of paper and taped next to the alarm keypad. The office carpet was dangerous, it was so worn out. So I asked the owner of the local home décor shop if we could have any used carpet they were going to throw away. She was great, and said they were putting new carpet in a home soon and we could have the carpet they pulled out. So we installed the used carpet. It looked kind of weird, because the traffic patterns worn on the carpet did not make sense based on the new installation. It was a source for lots of humor. After all, who would not savor having dirty white shag carpet in their office?

One day I got a call from a woman who was part of a corporate retreat at La Casa del Zorro, the local five star resort. She wanted me to talk about the park to her corporate classmates. So I went over to La Casa on a Sunday afternoon and discussed park issues with about twenty-five bigshots from the Herman Miller Corporation (a large office furniture corporation). I guess they were impressed that I would go over there on a Sunday afternoon (I don't think they had spent too many Sunday afternoons in Borrego Springs), because they kept asking me how they could help the park. I next met a few of them in my office, and the moment they walked into the office, they knew how they could help. They began by taking the passcode down from the alarm keypad, but then they asked if it would be alright if they redesigned the office. Since this is what they do as a Fortune 1000 company, I decided what the heck and gave them permission. They not only turned their designers loose, but the company wound up donating $70,000 worth of desks, counters, cubicle dividers, chairs, and so forth to the park. Our little story made it into their annual report that year. A great company. To thank them, I bought each of them a quart of raw apple cider and hid the bottles under the front seats of their cars.

I decided to go "out of the box" while leading this team building exercise for the executive staff at Herman Miller.

We have to go back and look at each other in the mirror...

Herman Miller had also hired a consultant to guide their retreat. At the end of the retreat, they had not used up all of their contracted time with the consultant, so they also donated eight hours for me to spend one-on-one with their high priced La Jolla consultant. He really helped me with how to handle some tricky management and personnel issues. The biggest takeaway for me was that I needed to be more clear and honest with staffers who were not performing. I had been trying to sugarcoat my treatment of these performance issues with gentle nudging. He suggested (correctly) that it would be better for me to be more direct, even though it was more painful for the staff person in the short term, and more uncomfortable for both of us. But it would be more productive, since they would really know what my expectations were. That way, the employee would "own" the responsibility for improving, since we would both be clear on the expectation, the current status, and the agreed upon road for improvement. It sounds easy looking back, and it was a great lesson.

"Throw strikes!" -- advice from my high school pitching coach whenever I would have a little control trouble during a game. Thank you, Captain Obvious...

When I arrived in Borrego, there were two major support groups (Non-profit organizations) for the park – the Anza-Borrego Foundation (ABF) and the Anza-Borrego Desert Natural History Association.

ABF was a land trust, set up to help acquire the many thousands of privately owned "inholdings" within the park boundary. As happened with many parks, the park was contemplated and established long before all the necessary lands were acquired; this provided many people the opportunity to purchase lands privately within the new park's boundaries. In 1967, ABF was established to try to acquire all these inholdings and transfer them to park ownership. ABF would only acquire lands that the owners wanted to sell or donate; neither they nor the state could condemn the lands. It was slow going, and even today there remain hundreds of owners of tens of thousands of acres within the park. Occasionally someone would come into the park office with a deed for property they had inherited and want to know where it was. Often, their property was on a very steep slope with no legal access. Usually they would wind up donating their real property to ABF, but sometimes you got the notion they really thought their ten or twenty acre parcel would be worth something more substantial.

After a couple of years, it became clear that ABF could do more than whittle away at inholdings. We started to discuss jointly the idea of working on "outholdings" – the lands adjacent to the park that would provide other benefits. In the late 80's and early 90's, State Parks, through the leadership of Rick Rayburn at Park Headquarters, started pushing the idea of "connectivity". That is, rather than continue to purchase parks as islands that would stand alone, we should be attempting to connect open space reserves. Really, in terms of resource management, it did not always matter whether you were connecting two reserves managed by the same agency; connecting a state park to a national forest, or a national park to a BLM reserve had great value for biodiversity as well.

The Really Big Bodacious Idea is to connect protected lands north of the US/Mexico border with those south of the border. The Peninsular Range that runs through Anza-Borrego, Cuyamaca, Palomar, Laguna, and Mt. San Jacinto south to the Sierra de Juarez range is the best candidate for this goal.

The ABF Board agreed, and we set our sights on some magnificent properties, such as Sentenac Canyon and the Lucky 5 Ranch. When we started doing our due diligence on land ownership, owners' willingness to sell, pricing, and sources of funds, we got really excited. There appeared to be some terrific opportunities. The early and mid-90's were a tough time economically for State Parks, but we decided to see how far we could get. We found out that the owner of Sentenac Canyon, in the magnificent San Felipe Valley, did want to sell. However, Diana Lindsay, the president of ABF at the time, told me she had talked to the land agent at Parks' Regional Office in San Diego, and he told her that although Sentenac was a priority for Dave Van Cleve, it was not a priority for the Department. That was a surprise to me, since I had discussed it with Regional Director Ken Jones, Resource Chief Rick Rayburn, and the Chief of Acquisition in Sacramento, Warren Westrup, and they all were very jazzed about and supportive of the project. So we decided to ignore the land agent and forged ahead. Ultimately, we acquired two large parcels in the Sentenac Canyon, including some incredible wetlands, a gallery cottonwood forest, and the site of an old stage station. Warren Westrup told me much later that the Sentenac acquisition was one of the top two most satisfying acquisitions of his career (along with Bodie), because of its biological importance and the fact that it was done when very little bond funding was available. Plus, it was a field driven project, unlike many priorities that are established for political reasons.

State Parks (Ken Jones and I) and the Anza-Borrego Foundation (Diana Lindsay and Ralph Singer) celebrate the opening of the beautiful Sentenac Canyon to the public.

It's as American as killing two birds with one apple pie...

One of the Sentenac wetlands was really choked with tamarisk trees, a non-native tree that uses a tremendous amount of groundwater. We were really dumb in this instance, because one of our guiding principles was to open new acquisitions to the public as soon as possible. I hated being accused of buying parkland and then "locking it up". I actually like locking it up; I just hate being accused of it. However, there is usually some period of time that is necessary to prepare property for public use. The large acquisitions are, in many instances, cattle ranches. So we need to reconfigure trails into a system that makes sense and is interesting to the park visitors. Also, surveys of natural and cultural resources need to be conducted, hazards need to be removed, signs installed, and restrooms built. Then there is the issue of staffing and funding the new property.

Anyway, we kind of rushed to construct a public use trail around the edges of the wetland, since it was a really good birding and hiking area. THEN we took out thousands of tamarisk trees. Although some current thought is that the removal of tamarisk does not release a lot of groundwater, I can personally attest that it does. We removed thousands of tamarisk, and soon our new trail was under water due to the release of vast amounts of groundwater. Hey, maybe I could use my SCUBA training to put in an underwater trail…

The Lucky 5 acquisition was trickier. I thought this ranch was important, since its addition to the ledger of permanently protected park lands would provide a wildlife corridor between the desert floor and the Cuyamaca Mountains. It would connect Anza-Borrego and Cuyamaca Rancho State Parks for the first time.

In the 70's, the Department was very close to completing the purchase of the Lucky 5 Ranch, when the contract was canceled and the funds diverted to the establishment of Colonel Allensworth State Historic Park in the Central Valley. (This also affected the purchase of the magnificent Rancho Guejito in the heart of San Diego County.) The owners of Lucky 5 vowed never to work with State Parks again, and who could blame them? In addition, the Lucky 5 acquisition never made it to the top of the Department's priority list, despite the support of the Regional Director and the Resource Management section. I think because it was not being threatened with imminent development, it was viewed as a project that could wait.

The offer was free gratis…

One day a major donor asked me to accompany him on a hike in Anza-Borrego to discuss a possible "major gift." Gee, let me think about that for one millionth of a second. On the hike, he asked me what my highest priority for acquisition in the Park would be, and I immediately told him, "The Lucky 5." He asked if ABF could do the deal, and I said they would probably hire some help, but that they did have the will and the enthusiasm. His donation was close to half of the acquisition cost, and we started a campaign to raise more private funds and government grants.

State Parks stayed totally out of the negotiations, since the owner still had a bad taste about the Department, and ABF hired Kevin Knowles, a conservation land broker, who handled almost everything. All went smoothly, and we finally had a connection between Anza-Borrego and Cuyamaca. A few years later, the adjacent, beautiful Tulloch Ranch was acquired as well to provide a significant corridor from Anza-Borrego to Cuyamaca Rancho. Who knows, with global climate change, Cuyamaca could be great bighorn sheep habitat some day!

Cuyamaca Rancho is one of the most beautiful units of the State Park System. Stonewall Peak provides a great location to view the Lucky 5 Ranch in the background, which connected, for the first time, Cuyamaca and Anza-Borrego Desert State Parks.

Another target for acquisition was the 3400-acre Vallecitos Ranch, which had a large population of the endangered least Bell's vireo, significant cultural resources, and the potential to re-establish a historical population of endangered bighorn sheep. Vallecitos was also the home of the largest collection of unassembled picnic tables, playground equipment, and used Cadillacs in eastern San Diego County. The owner, Norm Kanoff, collected some weird stuff, and was difficult to deal with. Every time we would meet with him to discuss acquiring his ranch, he appeared to be willing to sell but had an unrealistic idea of the value of the ranch and would always throw in a couple of weird conditions. For some reason, we would be required to remove the letter "V" from the English language, and I took that personally.

Norm died suddenly and unexpectedly, so at least the pressure on the letter "V" issue went away. I was in my office about a week later talking to Kevin Knowles, the land broker. I asked Kevin, "In your opinion, what is the appropriate amount of time we should wait before contacting Norm's widow, Claire Kanoff, and seeing if she might be a little more realistic about selling the Vallecitos Ranch?" Before Kevin could answer, the phone rang, and it was Claire. Before I could express condolences, she asked me, "Are you guys still interested in buying this pile of crap?" Of course, when the owner considers the asset a "pile of crap", that is good news for our side. I turned ABF and Kevin loose, and we were cutting the ribbon less than a year later.

For a while, towards the end of my career with State Parks, I was able to focus on some of these large acquisitions. There were about three years where the stars aligned, and we made some real progress. There was bond money available for acquisition; the state was actually solvent; there were some important properties whose owners became "willing sellers"; and the ABF board and staff were very willing and capable co-conspirators. I think too that a lot of my fellow district superintendents kind of soured on new acquisitions. In years past, a new major acquisition would be followed a year or two later with additional funds in the district support budget. That made sense – more land equals more work, so that should be supported with additional staff and support dollars. But more recently, the question from the Department of Finance was, "Are you going to be able to operate the additional real property with your existing budget?" If you answered "No", the acquisition would probably be denied. So you had to answer "Yes." Then the darn Department of Finance would remember that answer when you submitted your request for additional funding to support that acquisition.

I am getting up on my feedbox here...

There was one other odd circumstance. At that time, the Chief of Administration (Marsha Henderson), the Maintenance Chief (Keenen Sederquist), and the Chief Ranger (Lynn Rhodes), were all women. In addition, they were all experienced and at the top of their game. But the real topper of this circumstance was that they were all married and living apart from their spouses. Now this was not due to marital problems, but because of the previously mentioned problem with spouses finding meaningful work in Borrego Springs. So we had three talented women in a town with little to do, none of whom wanted a relationship other than that with their husband. Their outlet was...WORK. At the same time, the remarkable Linda Tandle was the executive director of the ABF. One of the main benefits was that I could really focus on acquisition work for a while, while these superstars ran the district operations and the land trust.

I learned one main lesson about how to negotiate on these real estate transactions: spend a lot of time figuring out what the motivation is for the person(s) with whom you are negotiating. It is not always money, or getting the best price. Some people truly want their land to be conserved permanently, so they may take less than market value to make that happen. Some are opposed to paying taxes, so they want to structure the deal in a manner that minimizes their tax burden. Some want to honor their family by having the park named for them. One guy I dealt with a lot believed that his father was a great negotiator, and he wanted to live up to that legacy. I learned to try to understand the other side. As author Steven Covey said, "Seek first to understand, and then be understood." Later, I had the opportunity to have lunch with Steven Covey, and he told me that not only could he not understand me, but it was unlikely that anyone could.

I came to enjoy the land acquisition side of the job. At Anza-Borrego, these were big deals, and there were opportunities not often found at most other state parks. Again, the downside is that support and staffing budgets did not keep pace. In fact, most properties acquired never did or will see a support budget. So the Department has to operate these new lands with existing funding. And recently, the existing funding has been slashed tremendously. It was through these deals that I started working with the staff of The Nature Conservancy. After I left state service in 2004, I spent nine years putting together deals for TNC. I had only two employers as an adult – State Parks and The Nature Conservancy, and people often ask me to compare them. I tell them that one is a large bureaucracy with cumbersome, stupid rules and policies, and the other is the California Department of Parks and Recreation.

I have a lot of black sheep in my closet...

Another tradition at Anza-Borrego is the annual bighorn sheep count. For over forty years, the park has been conducting a water-hole census of the endangered bighorn. In early July every summer, about eighty volunteers spread out to the known and suspected watering holes of the sheep and spend three days in the one hundred plus degree heat recording information on their sightings. They do it in July, not to torture the volunteers, but to be efficient about the effort. When temperatures near a hundred degrees, the sheep need to drink water at least every three days. That is why the count lasts three days. Also, the Sonoran Desert has monsoonal rains that are most common in August and September. In July, the dispersed water from winter rains has dried up and the monsoons have not arrived yet from the Gulf of California, so water sources are at their most concentrated level. The good news is that it is dry; the bad news is that it is VERY hot.

He was a wolf in cheap clothing...

There are three options for participating in the census. The first is to backpack in to a count site for the three days. Since it is so hot, you need to carry in a shade structure and support poles to construct a little viewing blind, along with your clothes, toiletry articles, and food. It is impossible to carry enough water for three days, so a water filter is required as well. My experience with filtering water was probably typical. The filter instructions tell you that the filter screens out microscopic particles, especially *giardia*, and that it is very safe. Then you stoop at the pool of stagnant green water that you are going to filter, pump a bunch of water through the filter, and then stare at the sticks and insects in your FILTERED water that seem to be a lot bigger than any *giardia* could be. You drink it, since you are really hot and thirsty. I am also thinking of trying the filter out on El Greco's elderberry wine.

I did three sheep counts by backpacking in, the most memorable of which was with good friends Howie Wier, Jim Dice, and Mike Kelley. When we arrived at the third grove of Borrego Palm Canyon, a rattlesnake let us know that this was HIS campsite. He was hidden in a bush. We set up camp anyway, stayed two nights, heard him buzz many times, but never saw him.

You can observe a lot just by watching...

You generally spend eight - nine hours per day trying to see sheep. We took turns being the main "glasser"; and there was plenty of opportunity to read, play games, or play tricks on Howie. Jim's favorite trick was to glue little sheep silhouettes on the lenses of Howie's binoculars. There was one cholla on a ridge north of our blind that I must have mistaken for a sheep dozens of times. Unfortunately, Kelley would not let me put it on our tally. I'll bet the volunteers at the adjacent blind counted it though...

One of my favorite count sites, Tubb Canyon.
Scanning for the elusive bighorn sheep.

At the same moment, Mike Kelley photographed
three ewes directly behind our count site. Arghh!

***You have to look at people as individuals and you can't just
throw a blanket over all of them...***

My first time backpacking in, I was frustrated near the end of the
third day, since I had not seen, heard, or even smelled a sheep. I
later learned that when the sheep count coordinator tells you
where you will be counting that year and mutters, "Biologically, it
is equally important to know where the sheep are NOT going," you
should IMMEDIATELY request a different count site. Finally I
heard a plaintive cry from down the canyon. I went to investigate,
very stealthily. The closer I got, the more plaintive the cries. I
finally reached a good vantage point, only to discover that the
cries were coming from a female of the human species, and she
and her ram boy were enjoying one of the large green stagnant

pools of water and its soft sandy bank. They were not wearing clothes, so I got out my official "Field Notes on Sheep Recordation" clipboard to take notes. I thought about asking her if she had ever considered becoming a ranger, but she appeared to be busy. Thank goodness, I had a really good pair of binoculars.

The worst part of the backpacking option is the water. No matter what you try, by the end of the third day you have cruddy water that is about the same temperature as the air – STINKIN' HOT! One of my main mammaries – oops, I mean memories; I was still thinking of the previous story – was hiking out to the end of the trail at the end of the count and thinking I would give almost anything for a bottle of cold, clear water. Well, I still would not switch for a smelly Chrysler Concorde. I did say "almost."

The second option of count sites is to drive into a base camp and set up camp. Then each day you hike to your observation site, and set up your blind. So there is still some hiking, but you can haul in a bunch of good water in your vehicle. There is no way to keep it cold for three days in that heat. I even tried dry ice one year, to udder failure. (Shoot, still trying to get rid of that visual…)

The third option (and I, like many others, went through the progression of options) is to get up early each of the three days and drive into your count site. At the end of the eight - nine hour day, drive back to civilization, known in this case by its code name – Borrego Springs. There are not many businesses open in Borrego in the summer, but there are enough to find a room, a restaurant, and, most importantly, a cold beer. After a year in state housing, I bought a house with a swimming pool. During the count, I would have people over every evening to swim, drink beer, and discuss how we USED to do one of the first two options. Then we would laugh and toast the options one and two people. Then we would go back to swimming and drinking more beer.

The goal is to get an idea of how the population of sheep is doing. Although there is error in the system (double counting the same sheep, missing some sheep), those errors are there every year and the staff tries to eliminate those. However, the count does provide trend data, and those data show that the population is generally improving in numbers.

I didn't know whether to wind the watch or bark at the moon...

One Sunday I got a call at home that Ranger Chaz had been bitten by a rattler and had been flown by helicopter to Palomar Hospital in Escondido. It turns out that Chaz had been giving a nature talk to some children about the rattlesnakes of Anza-Borrego Desert State Park. In a moment of, let's say, um, INSANITY, Chaz decided his talk would be really impressive if he showed the children a live rattler. And to really make his talk memorable, rather than show them the rattler in a cage, he decided to use the time-tested "hand-held" object method. Fortunately, Chaz did choose what the literature on reptiles called "the most docile" of the Park's four species of rattlesnakes – the Southern Pacific rattler. Unfortunately, the snake that Chaz captured had not read the chapter on "docility." Or maybe he had the same lit professor I had at UC Santa Cruz. Fortunately, Chaz had perfected the technique of holding this tame little snake behind the head and wowing the kids. Unfortunately, the snake had perfected the ability to spin around and bite the handler's index finger. To his credit, Chaz did not panic and throw the less-than-docile rattler in the direction of the kids. A helicopter was called in to "lifeflight" Chaz to the hospital in Escondido.

I drove to the hospital that afternoon to see Chaz. When I walked in, his first statement was, "There is no policy against what I did." I told him that, well, there WOULD be a policy in place by the next day; and while we could not possibly have a policy for everything, we kind of expected rangers, and all staff for that matter, to use good judgment.

I asked Chaz how his finger felt, and he said that when the snake bit him, it felt like a bee sting and really hurt. Then an hour later, it felt like he had hit his finger with a framing hammer as hard as he possibly could. Then another hour later, it REALLY started to hurt like a sumbitch.

He was treated with ten vials of antivenin, a large amount. Chaz went through treatment and therapy, but he eventually opted to have his index finger removed, due to the pain. Thereafter, in the office, it was hard to use the paper cutter without thinking of ol' three-finger Chaz.

Remember that America is still the best place to find the American dream…

In 1993, the Department went through yet another reorganization. Anza-Borrego Desert State Park was grouped with Cuyamaca Rancho, Palomar Mountain, Salton Sea, Picacho, Mt. San Jacinto, and Indio Hills to form the Colorado Desert District. The Colorado Desert is a part of the larger Sonoran Desert and included some of the best park units in the Department. The new district had a desert, the peninsular mountain range, the Colorado River, a sea…it was, without doubt, the most incredible district in the park system. It had the highest and lowest elevations of any state park units, the biggest river, the most biodiversity, the best collection of fossils (no, NOT the employees at Cuyamaca), and a terrific staff, not to mention the largest collection of unassembled picnic tables, playground equipment, and used Cadillacs in eastern San Diego County. Plus, I could now try to corner ninety-five percent of the market on whining. To my great fortune, I was chosen to be the superintendent of this monster district.

Unfortunately, combining these units into one district occurred during difficult times, so some employees were transferred against their will. Also, we really had to scramble to find equipment to meet all our needs. Each unit believed that it got screwed in the reorganization, and there was resentment that Anza-Borrego was now viewed as the favorite child. Borrego Springs became the home of the district office, and the new staff that were reassigned from the defunct regional office were also housed in Borrego Springs. These were delicate times, and we had to continue to operate the units, serve the public, and protect the resources. Somehow, I came to believe that Salton Sea had some extra computers compared to the need at the newly formed district office, and I asked Steve Horvitz, superintendent at the Sea, to transfer one of his PC's to the district. Steve told me in no uncertain terms that he would throw it in the Sea before he would give it to the district. Hey – another chance to show off my SCUBA skills? This may have been a hint that the staff at the Sea and at Picacho were among those who felt they had been screwed. Eventually, Steve and I wound up as good friends with a very respectful relationship.

Once Pandora has been squeezed out of the box, you can't put her back in again..

Have you ever gone backpacking in a tuxedo? I had to do it late one afternoon, and it was totally unplanned. The Mt. San Jacinto Winter Park Authority, a quasi-public agency, actually ran the Palm Springs Aerial Tramway. The tram is a weird duck, since most of the ascension goes through (above) the state park. Almost from the start, their ridership revenues never matched projections, and they were in debt for decades. Finally, in the late 90's, they were able to pay off their loans, and a celebration was planned. They decided to make it a "black tie" event, so my wife and I got dressed up for the occasion – she in a beautiful dress and me in a tuxedo.

Rick Campbell, the park superintendent, was also there in formal wear. During the cocktail hour, a tramway supervisor approached Rick and me and told us that there was a park visitor in physical distress in Long Valley, near the mountain station of the tram. I asked Rick who was on duty, and he told me he had given the entire staff the afternoon off. So Rick and I were it as far as trained first responders.

We walked down the trail into Long Valley, and at the bottom of the ramp we saw a man and woman in their twenties with their backpacks off. As we approached, the woman asked the man if he thought that they should call his wife. Just another day in the forest! He almost screamed "NO!" We evaluated the couple, and it was soon evident that the man was suffering from acute altitude sickness. The woman was fine, other than her apparently nutso suggestion to call THE WIFE. He could hardly move and was having difficulty breathing. The fastest remedy for altitude sickness is, um, to get to lower altitude. Usually, in the mountain wilderness areas, this is a very arduous and time consuming process. But we were a short hike from the upper tramway terminal, which could get him 6,000' lower in fifteen minutes, and from there they could drive another 2,000' lower in another ten minutes or so. We decided to cheat and use the tramway and not hike him and his friend the fifteen miles to Idyllwild. Since he could not carry his pack, Rick and I put his and his partner's backpacks on over our tuxedos, and hiked up to the mountain station, while his partner helped him walk up the ramp.

Probably not a photo often seen in outfitter catalogues!

Also, since the couple had hiked over to the tram from Idyllwild, they had no car at the valley station. He totally recovered from altitude sickness once he reached the valley station, but I never heard if he recovered from telling his wife she needed to pick up his "partner" and him and give them a ride back to Idyllwild.

He doesn't have half a brain to piss in...

In the late-90's, the fifty-year old operating agreement between the Mt. San Jacinto Winter Park Authority and the Department of Parks and Recreation was about to expire, and I was tasked with writing and negotiating a new agreement. Since the tramway had started operating in the early 60's, the Parks Department had paid the tram authority over $14,000 per year. You read that right; the property owner was essentially paying the "concessionaire." As you can imagine, their board members liked this pay structure and did not want to tinker with it. Ken Jones was in Sacramento as the Department's Deputy Director for Operations, and he had dealt with tramway issues as a Regional Director and as a District Superintendent. I had worked at the park as a ranger, ecologist, and now as District Superintendent. I did the regular meetings and the drafting of the agreement, and Ken would come down as needed to provide support. You could call me, "Bad Cop."

The meetings with the tramway authority were comical, in a way. There were usually six or seven board members there, along with their general manager and their attorney. On our side of the table, well, it was just ol' Dave. The first thirty minutes of every meeting were filled with their folks ranting about how stupid state managers were and how poorly the state was run. "Nothing personal, of course, Dave." So I started coming to meetings thirty minutes late, and told them they could just spend that time ranting without me present. I guess they eventually got the picture. Ken and I were eventually able to "Turn the Queen Mary" around, and the tramway now pays some its revenues to the state. There were a lot of other issues dealt with, but the basic premise of which way the money flowed was the main one. Although this was not a particularly exciting or amusing negotiation, I regard it as one of the best, and quietest, achievements of my career.

Some time later, the general manager for the tram asked to meet with me. He informed me that the tram was planning on installing new, larger tram cars, and that Cal OSHA was requiring them to provide for a wider corridor for the tram cars on their journey up and down the mountain. Since the tram cars came close at a couple of points to rock outcroppings, they would need to remove these outcroppings. I asked him what his timetable was, and he said "Two weeks". Ever so innocently, I asked "Two weeks until what?", and he replied "Until we start blasting rock." At that point I think that my coffee actually passed upwards through my nose; I started choking and said, "Let me get this straight. You want to blast two thousand tons of granite out of a STATE PARK, in the middle of habitat for a federally listed endangered species (bighorn sheep), you have not started the environmental review process, and you want to start in two weeks?" It was no surprise that he was not the general manager for much longer.

They couldn't see that there was some straw on the camel's back...

I was in the office one day, and the dispatcher yelled at me to come listen to the radio traffic. I got to the front office just in time to hear a ranger say over the radio, "Oh no...the deputy sheriff just shot the hostage!" From everything I remembered from my training, you were supposed to shoot the bad guys, not the hostage. But of course, I did not have all the facts yet. Once things calmed down, we found out that it was not a hostage, but an OSTRICH that had been shot. Gee, that made a lot more sense and was MUCH easier to understand. Perhaps we should have had our Australian-speaking ranger translate for us. It turns out some town resident had brought their pet ostrich to (what passes for) downtown Borrego Springs. They did not have their ostrich on a leash, because, naturally, their ostrich was a good ostrich and was under voice command. Further, there were no signs stating that ostriches must be kept on leash. I suspect this animal may have been the product of a pitbull/ostrich tryst, for he got very aggressive and start attacking innocents in Borrego Springs. You can picture it – he kept striking at people with those long legs and talons. The rangers and deputies were called in, and they asked the owner to give the ostrich the command to stick his head in the sand, but apparently they had not perfected that one yet. He could not even "Play Dead." Finally, in an obvious case of suicide by cop, the ostrich attacked a deputy sheriff. Thirteen shots later, the ostrich lay dead. One of the hardest things I ever had to do was inform the ostrich's family that their father had been killed. "Sorry for your lostrich." An investigation is still pending, and the officer remains on administrative leave.

When I think back, it seems like there were many more unbeaten teams at the beginning of the season last year...

Being a ranger is not all fun, of course. After thirty-plus years, Jim Burke was getting ready to retire from the Department. We took one final tour of the magnificent backcountry of Cuyamaca Rancho State Park. At one point, I said, "Hey, let's make a list of all the really cool things we did during our careers." After we completed the list, we agreed to burn it, since it was not really fair that we had had so much fun at work. Jim was great to work with, I mean, it was great to work with Jim, who was great, oh screw it... Halfway through a staff meeting, he would pretend to sneeze and a huge plastic glob of snot would fly on to the conference table, or he would put in googly eyes, or HEY, pretend to cut off a finger or two using the paper cutter. I heard tales about him wearing ape masks in the campground making field collections. The business of managing parks can be stressful, and it is so delightful to work with people that make it fun.

He also helped me with the lesson that you can't control everything that happens to you, but you can determine what your reaction will be. I used to barf on his uniform shirt when he would say that, just to see how he would react. Of course, Jim was wearing the shirt at the time, unlike my experience. He got pretty good at staying calm.

Jim Burke and I at Cuyamaca, going over the list of fun things we
did in our careers. Jim listed "Hugging Dave" in his top three.
He also told me I should wear my Stetson lower on my head.

No use beating him over the head with a dead horse...

When I arrived at Anza-Borrego, I had to adjust to the heat, the
small town status, and the people. One of the phrases I kept
hearing from park staff was, "We do things a little differently in

Borrego." I soon learned that sometimes that was good, and sometimes that was bad.

John Curdlicker, one of the editors of the local newspaper (The Borrego Sun) would spell my name incorrectly every time he wrote a story about the park. And it was different each time. At first, I thought he was doing it intentionally. After all, my dad had been the editor of a small town newspaper, and his attention to spelling and grammar was legendary. He and my mother, an English teacher, would not allow any improper conjugations in our house while I was up growing. For example, my brothers and I were never allowed to end a sentence with a preposition. Let's say that I would slide into grammarian purgatory with a sentence like, "What did you do that for?" One of us would have to immediately (OH NO...a split infinitive!) mutter a word like "jerkface" or "buttkisser" so that the ultimate word of the sentence was not a preposition. Anyway, back to Mr. Curdlicker. My irritation was relieved a tad when I started to notice that he often misspelled his OWN NAME on the photo credits. I started calling him John CRUDLICKER, to point out his error, but he never caught on. His other little trick would be to criticize me or the park but call it something else. As an example, he would say something to me like, "Hey, I noticed that dress really makes your butt look fat," or "I see where you went over budget by eight thousand percent last year." My face would turn red and I would start to bristle, and he would come back with "This is not a criticism, merely an observation." My parents had taught me to stay always on the high road, though. So I told him that MY observation was that he was a buttkissing jerkface. Then I would tell him how to spell those words. Actually, my journalist dad told me never to get into a spat with someone who buys ink by the barrel and newsprint by the ton. It took until I moved to Borrego Springs for me to understand what he was getting at...

I wasn't living under my parents' house anymore...

I moved into state housing for the first year, a cinder block home next to the maintenance shop. One nice thing about cinder block is that it is a terrific absorber and storer of heat; in the summer, this means that the west facing rear wall of the house becomes an absolute beast of high temperatures and spends the evening spreading that hot glow throughout your home. The house also had cockroaches and scorpions. Ken Jones told me that rubber shower shoes were the best tool for cockroaches – strong and supple enough to snap a cockroach to death on the wall, but not so heavy that the cockroach would splatter on the wall. The roach would die and fall to the floor without leaving a yucky mess. The things we can learn from our Regional Directors! More than once, a nighttime visit walk across the living room was rewarded by a sting from a scorpion. I learned to treat it like a bee sting. Apply ice and check back in the morning. These little guys were not poisonous, so their presence and their presents were annoying but not fatal (much to the dismay of some of the staff and townspeople.)

He tears everything up like a bull in China...

When I arrived at work, the maintenance staff could not wait to tell me about one of their supervisors, Randy. Randy had been given a two-step promotion to Worker II at Borrego, and was still on probation. Apparently, the hiring staff at Anza-Borrego had never called to check references on Randy, because the staff at Randy's former park kept calling me to ask how he was doing. Then they would laugh like crazy, and say wild things like, "Thank God you guys never check references!"

A carpenter is the dog on the lowest rung of the totem pole...

I am pretty sure that Randy never passed one of the Department's terrific maintenance skills classes. Employees that want to improve their skills as an electrician, plumber, carpenter, or other tradesperson can pretty much get to the journey level at the Department's expense by taking these classes. The first thing that staff pointed out was the duplex outlets around the office – the regular electric plugs used for appliances, lights, and vibrators. Dripping from almost every plastic outlet cover were large globs of dried glue. I tried to unscrew the cover plate to see what was going on, but there was no screw. I pried off the cover with a screwdriver, which had been glued on, and to my surprise, there were big globs of glue inside the junction box as well. For some reason, Randy abhorred the idea of using screws around electricity (I could think of no other conclusion), and would just get out his glue gun and have at it. One would think that wiping off the excess glue at the end of the job might hide his incompetence or screwtaphobia, but no. Maybe he was proud of his work, who knows? After all, the plugs worked….occasionally.

But the maintenance staff got their biggest kick out of the drinking fountain Randy was asked to repair in the campground. The drinking fountain fixture was inoperative, and Randy was successful at removing the offender. He could not locate (or take the time to purchase) a replacement fixture, but he did find a hose nozzle lying around, and used copious amounts of glue to affix that to the drinking fountain. He also made sure to glue the nozzle open in the "hard jet" rather than "fine spray" position. We had an unusual number of bloody nose incidents from campers and vociferous complaints regarding that fountain before competent staff realized what Randy had done and corrected it. They were sure to take pictures first.

That's using your head for something besides a footstool…

A couple of years later, I saw Randy at a gas station in Escondido. Now he was wearing the uniform of his new employer – the San Diego Wild Animal Park – one of those zoos where the animals are in very large enclosures that mimic their natural habitat. His uniform said "Ranger", and he appeared to be wearing a sidearm. I tried to get a good look at his weapon (without him seeing me). The good news is that it was NOT a glue gun; the bad news is that it was a .38 caliber revolver! I guess State Parks was not alone in not checking references. Every time thereafter that I would hear of an exotic zoo animal meeting an untimely and suspicious death, I would think of Randy.

We will burn that bridge when we get to it…

One of the most difficult jobs as a manager arises when it becomes necessary to attempt to change public recreational behavior. This change may be due to the damage that is occurring to the park's resources, the likelihood of such damage, the conflict between different types of recreation, or other reasons. Road closures, banning alcohol, hours of operation, restricting use on trails, and closures of parts of the park are examples of this. Another difficulty occurs when the park acquires new tracts of land where the public or certain user groups suddenly have to operate under park rules.

Sometimes you have to draw a sword in the sand...

In the early 70's, President Nixon made the Marine Corps at Camp Pendleton lease a lot of its beachfront property to the Department to create San Onofre State Beach. The old Highway 101 became a linear, bluff top campground and day use parking area. Far trickier was the lease of the "Surfing Beach" to the Department. For decades prior to this change, the Marines had allowed the San Onofre Surf Club to use and operate this excellent surfing beach. Their rules of operation were slightly different than those of the Department. When Dick Troy, Ken Simmons, and I were at San Onofre, this changeover was still very recent, and the "members" of the Surf Club were not happy. No longer could they build big bonfires or run their dogs in the surf. "Dogs run free; why can't we?" were Bob Dylan's dumbest lyrics ever, from the point of view of rangers. Gee, sir; I have never heard that one before. Wait; even worse was Buffalo Springfield's "I Shot the Sheriff," which seemed to emanate from every dirtbag campsite in the 70's. That certainly had a calming effect on patrol rangers. But what made members of the San Onofre Surf Club really miserable was that the state park now allowed the damned public into what once was THEIR exclusive surf beach.

Sometimes I feel like I am swimming uphill against the grain...

Later, when I was assigned to Ranch del Oso (RDO), the coastal connection for Big Basin Redwoods State Park, I went through this again. Another recent addition to the Park System, RDO had a beautiful wide beach through which Waddell Creek flowed to the ocean. It had been privately owned prior to its transfer to State Parks. The previous owners had no means of really restricting use on the beach, so it had become a popular, but unauthorized, off-roading beach. One of my jobs was to eliminate the use of motor vehicles on the beach. We had a heavy equipment operator on staff, and I got him to help me physically make it as difficult as possible for vehicles to get from the beach parking lot on to the sand. I have come to learn that there is no more creative mind than that of the off-roader who REALLY wants to get somewhere he has been told is off limits. Between the physical barriers, the plethora of signs (I used paper signs to save money, since no sign lasted more than twenty-four hours), and a whole lot of written citations, we finally brought this usage under control. I figure it takes a generation to really effect the change. You have to get past the "I used to do this with my Dad and Grandpa" phase. I still enjoy visiting Rancho del Oso – truly a beautiful park unit.

There will definitely be a few feathered ruffles over this...

The ultimate changes in use were at Anza-Borrego, however, particularly vis-à-vis the off-roading activity. Besides the removal of green stickers from the park in 1987, there were other major battles. For decades, motor vehicles had been able to go from the town of Anza to the town of Borrego Springs – about eighteen miles of very rugged terrain. The primitive road went through Coyote Canyon and Coyote Creek, through several palm/willow oases, and the torturous "Turkey Track." There were some organized vehicle cavalcades that did this route, and people did it in both directions. Like a lot of things, when it was just a few vehicles a year, there were probably few impacts. However, as the technology of off-road vehicles improved, as population grew, and as word spread, the usage of this route greatly increased. Besides its recreational attractiveness, Coyote Canyon was remarkable in its natural and cultural importance. Home to the endangered desert bighorn sheep and least Bell's vireo, Coyote Canyon also was habitat for palm oases and numerous sensitive species. It was the route that Juan Bautista de Anza, for whom the park is named, traversed twice in the late 18th century on his route to the Bay Area. And, due to its perennial surface water, the canyon was heavily used by the Cahuilla Indians for centuries.

He knew how to butter his nest...

In the lower part of the canyon, the road went right up the creek for a couple of miles. As resource protection concerns grew, it became clear that this motor vehicle use was damaging the natural and cultural values of the lower creek and its environs. I thought the Department came up with a reasonable solution – it would, at park expense, build a "bypass" road around the wetlands known as "Lower Willows." That way, motor vehicle usage of the canyon could continue, including through traffic from Borrego Springs to Anza. Well, lawsuits were filed, loud public meetings were held, and even the Director visited the park. He came up with a really clever phrase, referring to the local endangered avian species as "the LAST Bell's vireo." Gee, sir; I have never heard that one before. Another memorable phrase was that of the litigants – that building a bypass road around Lower Willows was the stupidest idea they had ever heard.

It may take several years to restore chaos after this lawsuit is settled...

One thing I learned as a resource ecologist was that the lawsuits filed by opponents of proposed actions by the parks were filed under the provisions of the California Environmental Quality Act, or CEQA. That did not seem right, that actions designed to PROTECT the environment were being challenged under the law that was created to PROTECT the environment. But that is the way the legal systems works, and I soon realized that I had to know and understand CEQA as well as or better than the litigants. And, more importantly, I had to ensure that the steps required by the law were rigorously followed. I beat that lesson into staff constantly as well. The lawsuits filed to challenge environmental protection proposed actions were based on whether we had followed the law – not whether the proposal actually had merit. Know the details of CEQA law; follow the details of CEQA law – that was our mantra. We were 11-0 in lawsuits.

INDEED!

That really gets my dandruff up, especially after we pulled their bacon out of the fire...

The bypass road was created, and nearly thirty years later it serves to help protect the resources of lower Coyote Canyon. In the ten years after the bypass action, however, it became increasingly clear that the presence of motor vehicles in Middle Willows, a smaller yet important wetland oasis a couple of miles farther up the canyon, were also being negatively impacted by motor vehicle traffic. Unfortunately, it was not physically possible to build a bypass around Middle Willows. Actually, I guess, it is

115

possible to build a bypass almost anywhere, but in this case it would be a major engineering feat. Also, the only areas where a bypass could be engineered in were important in terms of natural and cultural resource protection, and the damage created by the bypass would rival or exceed the impacts being mitigated by avoiding Middle Willows traffic. Paul Jorgensen was tasked with creating the Coyote Canyon Management Plan, which addressed several management issues in that beautiful desert riparian corridor. The plan recommended the permanent closure of Middle Willows to motor vehicle traffic, which also meant that through-traffic would be eliminated. Well, lawsuits were filed, loud public meetings were held, and the Chief Deputy Director even visited the park. For some odd reason, that idiot visited Coyote Canyon without telling Park staff, but he was chauffeured up the canyon by the Superintendent of Ocotillo Wells State Vehicular Recreation Area. I am sure that he received an unbiased commentary on the germane issues. I do not often get angry, but that "secret" visit really pissed me off.

You hit it right on the nail...

Part of our strategy, which Ron McCullough had taught me, was to build broad support, not only in the chain of command, but with elected officials, the press, and partners. I flew to Sacramento for meetings with key partners. Ken Jones was now the Deputy Director for Operations, and Ken had worked at Anza-Borrego as Chief Ranger, so he knew the park well. We were about to walk downstairs in the Resource Building to meet with the Department of Fish and Game (DFG) when Ken dusted off his file on the issue. I asked him if he wanted me to make the presentation (we were trying to get DFG to write a letter of support), since I was living and breathing this controversy, and Ken probably had a dozen or so issues going of equal importance and controversy. Ken said no, "I got this." Ken laid out the issue for DFG in about twenty minutes, and I have to admit he did a beautiful job without missing one key point. I was impressed not only by his grasp of the issues but his ability to make a perfectly organized presentation of a complex issue, seemingly off the top of his head. I guess that is why he was Deputy Director, and I was STILL out in the desert whining.

People will blow smoke and mirrors at you...

One of the amusing proposals from the off-roaders was that now they REALLY supported the idea of a bypass road for Middle Willows. Ten years earlier, a bypass road was a horrible idea. I guess in comparison to NO access, a bypass was now the smartest idea they had ever heard. The management plan and management actions were eventually approved, and the lawsuits were decided in favor of the proposed actions. One weird thing about the lawsuits is that you seldom know when they are really over. There are time periods prescribed by law for challenges, and also for any appeals. So instead of there being a "champagne moment" – HEY WE WON!!, one day you get a call from the DPR legal office saying, "Well, we think the date has passed for filing any further appeals, and to the best of our knowledge no further appeals were filed, so tentatively we believe that it is possible that we may no longer be in a position of expecting further appeals." Wow – let's celebrate THAT, um, well, tentatively at least.

He has always been a real stench park supporter...

On the Coyote Canyon issue, the Board of Supervisors of San Diego County decided to weigh in. I got a call from the chief of staff of one of the supervisors, and he told me the Board had calendared a hearing to decide whether they would oppose the Department's proposed action there. I told him the Board did not really have a role in this decision, and he informed me that under the principle of "Home Rule", the San Diego County Board might indeed have some jurisdiction on this issue. I asked him to explain Home Rule to me, since I was just a dumb state manager. He told me that it was a national movement to return decision making to local jurisdictions, since the federal and state governments did not have the local knowledge and expertise found on local legislative bodies. I asked him to send me a copy of the proposed County resolution, and he faxed it to me right away. The resolution had eighteen "whereases" that led to the "therefore be it resolved." And the resolution basically opposed the Department's proposal to close Middle Willows to motor vehicle traffic. I made a copy, marked it up, and sent it back to the chief of staff. I told him that I had no role in opposing the Board's desire to pass a resolution, just as the Board did not have a role in our action other than making its feelings known. However, in order to avoid public embarrassment, he might want to change the wording of fifteen of the eighteen "whereases", since each of those fifteen contained factual errors. Further, the Board should be aware that Middle Willows is located in Riverside County, not San Diego County. Therefore, if San Diego County actually did invoke "Home Rule" and claim jurisdiction over this action, it might want to inform the Riverside County Board of Supervisors of its predatory actions. The resolution passed unchanged. Local knowledge and expertise indeed!

The Chief Ranger really turned it around on that issue; he did a complete 360...

Before the decision was implemented, Chief Ranger John Quirk came into my office. He told me that the entire Visitor Services staff, including him, thought that the proposal to close Middle Willows to motor vehicles was not a good one, and that it would be difficult on the staff. A few minutes later, I was able to come down from the ceiling and tell him that I was sorry that I would ever ask the staff to handle anything DIFFICULT! I thanked him for his input and told him I hoped he would always feel comfortable coming in and expressing a different opinion than mine. I then assigned him the task of cleaning the glue off all the electrical outlets in the office.

Actually, what really happened was that I told John that I realized it would be a difficult task, but that it was absolutely the right thing to do. None of these actions was easy, but that does not mean they should not be undertaken. It was our job as managers to have the courage to do the right thing. To John's credit, he came in six months later, after we had implemented the action, and told me that I had been right – it was the right thing to do. I always admired him for that.

It sounded like a one-eyed cat playing the banjo in a seafood store...

I kind of make light of a lot these issues, but at the time they were very stressful. People hear that you work for State Parks, and they think that means a very laid back job and career, for some reason. So it helps to look for ways to have fun off the job. One day, Robie Evans, who worked at the Borrego Springs Bank, called and asked if I would like to be in a musical theater production in Borrego Springs. It was a small role, and I thought it would be fun. So I said sure. The next year, she asked me to be the lead in "The Music Man", which was quite a step up. I quickly found out that Borrego Springs is just big enough to have a theater company, and just small enough that everyone who tries out gets a role in the play. You can imagine how many middle-aged white males there are in a town that small that can sing, dance, and act. After my audition, they said the total was still zero. Actually, Jon Muench was also in "The Music Man", and he did have a lot of talent. He wound up being in a couple of dozen plays, and still acts in productions in Idaho. My first few roles in THE THEATER were as a Nazi, a flim flam man/con artist, an angry king, a nerdy bureaucrat, and a very mean, stern, and rigid father figure. The staff at the park had a great joke – "When are you going to land a role that actually requires you to ACT? So far, these are all type cast roles!" Finally, I was cast as a dancing florist in "Little Shop of Horrors." THAT shut them up! It also shut up the audiences of "Little Shop." I also did not think their joke was very funny...

My favorite role was the King in "The King and I." My lovely wife Mary was the "I", and we had a blast doing that show in Borrego Springs. She is so talented that some audience members forgot that the show title is NOT "I and the King." I had them flogged. An out-of-town producer happened to see the show and asked us to take the production back East, so we did a short run in, um, Brawley. Hey, IT IS east of Borrego Springs...

"Shall We Dance" at the <u>King and I</u>, 1997

He may be the world's only living brain donor...

One of the weirdest off-roader contacts our staff had was when a local city councilman, Bob Monroe, decided to drive into an unauthorized area of the park – Clark's Dry Lake -- one Sunday afternoon. Now Anza-Borrego was not part of Monroe's district, but he drove out with some friends, ignored several "Area Closed to Motor Vehicles" signs, and did a bunch of "donuts" in the dry lake bed. One of the park's rangers saw this and made contact. Monroe claimed not to have seen any signs, but the rangers at Anza-Borrego are all very good at tracking vehicles, and it was clear that Monroe and his friends had gone right past the "closed area" signs. So the ranger issued him a citation. When it came time to fill in the license plate information, the ranger noticed that the truck had an unusual plate – a plate that identified Monroe as an elected official. (No, it did not say "DH". Based on Monroe's actions and attitude, though, we thought it should.) Monroe told the ranger that he was a former Marine, that he had walked enough as a marine to last a lifetime, and that he was going to drive everywhere from now on. I hope he had a nice drive to the courthouse.

I got a call at home later that afternoon from the ranger, and he told me what had happened and asked if he (the ranger) were in trouble. After hearing the story, I told him that yes, he was in trouble. He asked why, since it seemed pretty straightforward. I said that with a misdemeanor committed in his presence, he had the right to make a physical arrest and transport Monroe to jail. Then I told him that, seriously, he had done the right thing, and that I would need to make some calls. We might catch some heat, but if I were Monroe I would hope to keep this quiet.

Unfortunately, the entire senior staff of the Department was at an "off-site" retreat all weekend, doing some planning. Also, it was at some remote park without cell phone service. So all my messages to the Regional Director, the Director, and all of the Director's staff went unanswered and unreturned all day Sunday. I wanted to be sure the Director heard from me before he heard from Monroe Monday morning about what had transpired. The Chief Deputy Director finally returned home late Sunday in Sacramento and returned my call. I thought the Department handled it well. They were glad to get the information early and never tried to get me or the ranger to back off or void the citation. I am sure the Marines are proud.

We do things a little differently in Borrego...

One afternoon we heard that a small airplane had landed next to the Wells Fargo Bank in "downtown" Borrego Springs. That sounded odd, since there was no airfield next to the bank, so we decided to check it out. Maybe Wells Fargo had installed a "fly-through ATM" but the pilot had forgotten his PIN. Fortunately for The Borrego Sun, the newspaper office was about one hundred yards from the bank, so their team of crack reporters jumped on it. The other decidedly odd thing about this unscheduled arrival was that there were no people in the plane — no pilot and no passengers. The truth had a hard time keeping up with the rumors and supposition on this story, and I am not sure the entire truth was ever known. For a while, the hot rumor was that some guy was seen getting into a rented plane in Carlsbad — the same plane that landed in Borrego, with two large suitcases. And we knew that the suitcases were NOT in the plane when it crashed. Further, this guy had had financial and marital problems, so people concluded that he had cooked up this elaborate scheme to disappear and not leave a trace. Maybe he had stashed a car at a remote airfield in the desert, took his valuables, important papers, and some clean underwear in two suitcases, got into a plane in plain view in Carlsbad to throw people off, then flew from Carlsbad to the desert airstrip and loaded his suitcases into the car, took off again, put the airplane on autopilot, parachuted out of the plane near the remote airstrip, then he drove to Mexico...well, you get the picture. Pretty fanciful conjecture. The FAA was able to determine that the plane had kind of, um, rambled around the skies over Borrego Springs for several minutes before heading for the bank, but searches for clues, people, or underwear underneath the flight path were fruitless. For two years, no one had a clue what had happened to the pilot, and the estranged wife had no idea what had happened to her husband. Finally, the body of the pilot was found up in a grapefruit tree in town. We will probably never know what really happened, although the discovery of his remains led to speculation that, just perhaps, his underwear fell out of his suitcase in midair, blew out of the plane but got snagged on the plane's rigging, and the pilot was reaching out as far as he could for the underwear with his cheek mashed against the window, when he saw some ripe grapefruit on a tree nearby and thought "I bet I could get me one of those NICE Borrego grapefruits," and the rest is history...

Well, that doesn't cut any ice with me...

Commercial filming always seems to cause issues in parks. There has always been some tension between the field and the Governor's office over filming, particularly movies and TV shows. I get the theory – filming production can bring a lot of revenue to the state and to local businesses, and lots of other states and cities are trying like crazy to "woo" film shoots to their locations for financial reasons. We could not charge them fees, other than to be reimbursed for direct expenses and to have a park monitor on site. However, the film companies put a lot of strain on park staff and, in many cases, on park resources. And they often wanted to do things that normal park visitors are simply not allowed to do.

That really puts the mustard on the rocks...

One film director was very creative. He wanted to drive a car over the side of Montezuma Grade, the steep, curving highway that rises dramatically out of Borrego Springs. Further, he wanted to have the car explode into flames upon impact after its aerial trip through the desert. Of course, this would not be permitted in the Park. Where this guy got imaginative was that he found out there was a small inholding (privately owned land within the park boundary), and his plan became to land the car on this inholding and then have it explode. Very "out of the box." The answer was still very "No." We were never convinced that the aerial trajectory plan was accurate; also, he had to begin the "flight" in the park. I swear, only at Anza-Borrego could some of these issues arise.

Another director was shooting an episode of "The X Files", a story of aliens interacting with government agents on earth. They wanted to use my office, which was fine. When I got to the office the next day, there was a triangular shape burned into the carpet in my office. I called the director in and asked him what had happened. He called in his equipment guy, who said they did not have any piece of equipment that could have made that "brand" in my carpet. I told them that, well, it was not there the previous day when I left the office. We finally agreed that it must have been caused by aliens. They said they would repair it, of course, and asked if I knew the number of the "dye lot" for the carpet so they could make a perfect color match. Let's see, the dye lot for forty-year old dirty white shag carpet. I must have left that note in my other shirt....

He'll definitely be having surgery since the MRI showed cartridge problems in his knee...

We did have one "officer involved shooting" when I was at the Colorado Desert District. Some guy decided to rob the Borrego Springs Bank in the town of Borrego, and he brandished a handgun during the robbery and pistol-whipped one of the bank employees. Then he realized that there were not too many hiding places nearby, since it was a DESERT, and he started driving towards Tamarisk Grove. Since the bank employees saw him get into his car, and there is only one road heading south out of town, and visibility averages, oh, a hundred miles or so, it was pretty easy for the two deputy sheriffs, two CHP officers, and eight park rangers to spot him trying to escape.

He came out of that one smelling like a bandit...

One quick-thinking deputy spike-stripped the highway near Tamarisk Grove, and the bad guy's car slammed to a halt. His judgment got even worse than that of Butch and Sundance in the final scene of their movie, for this guy started firing his gun at a whole bunch of cops nearby. It ended badly for the bad guy, but all the officers who shot back did not feel too good either. This was probably a real case of suicide by cop.

The rise in the unemployment figures is due to a higher number of people being out of work...

We had a terrific local State Senator, Denise Ducheny. Before becoming a Senator, she actually served on the board of the Anza-Borrego Foundation. I asked her one time if she wanted to visit one of the other parks in her District – Picacho State Recreation Area. Picacho is a beautiful park on the shore of the Colorado River. By the time the river gets this far, it has been controlled by many dams, and it runs about two - three knots. It is a great spot for a half-day float trip. We had an outfitter lined up who would take a bunch of us, including the Senator and her husband, up the river twelve miles with several kayaks and paddles. Then we would float back down to the docks in Picacho and would have the opportunity to see the beautiful desert and river and discuss park issues. They were going to drive out from San Diego Thursday morning; we would float the river that afternoon, and then have a barbecue that evening. They had to get back to San Diego Friday afternoon. We kept waiting and waiting most of Thursday. I had sent them driving directions on how to get to the park, which was off the beaten path, but on well-identified dirt roads.

Picacho State Recreation Area (it should be a State Park) is one of those little known and seldom visited parks that is a true gem. Floating down the Colorado River was a great joy. I only wish I had been more successful in getting the stinkin' burros out of there. Not sure here if I am in CA looking west to AZ, or...

He started cooking his goose deeper and deeper -- one brick short of the whole nine yards...

Unfortunately, the aide who was accompanying them decided to "Mapquest" the route. Just guessing here, but this may have been in the days before Mapquest had all the bugs worked out. We finally heard from the Marines at the air station in Yuma that they had been doing some maneuvers in a helicopter and saw a motorhome stuck in the sand out in the middle of the desert. They said they landed to offer assistance, and there was a Senator in the group with the stranded motorhome. Of course, this got the Marines busy, since they probably figured it was either US Senator Feinstein or Boxer. They finally got it straight and called us. They vectored our ground units to the site of the motorhome, and they were great about helping us put rocks under the RV tires until we were able to get the RV back on solid ground. Mapquest had sent Senator Ducheny and her party on a whole bunch of unmarked dirt roads, and they had gotten hopelessly lost. We had to scrap the float trip, but we recovered with a good barbecue. Best of all, it was HER STAFF that screwed up – not us. I wonder if that aide still has a job...

I didn't have two minutes to rub together...

One of our goals in inviting Senator Ducheny out to Picacho was to show her the problems caused by the non-native burros. Not only did the burros drive out the local population of desert bighorn sheep, but they really bothered the campers at Picacho. Burros are noisy, crap everywhere, chew up picnic tables, and are just a general nuisance. However, they are protected, as are wild horses, by federal law. We hoped that Senator Ducheny would contact her federal counterparts and get us some help from the Bureau of Land Management (BLM.) The red tape that federal agencies can throw in front of progress is truly amazing. I think the BLM wins the first place prize for bureaucratic blizzardry, followed closely by The Nature Conservancy, then State Parks. After fourteen meetings with BLM on burro removal, only six burros had been removed from the park. Later, when I worked on pig removal with an inter-agency task force, we held twenty-four meetings with only a few pig removals. I think the standard should be at least one vertebrate pest removed for every meeting held. I am way behind on meeting that standard at this point.

Pull over; I cannot do my job at 55 miles per hour...

I was heading to a ten a.m. "burro" meeting with BLM in El Centro one day with Jim Dice, Mark Jorgensen, and Paul Jorgensen – our "A" team of ecologists. Paul was driving, and it is normally a ninety-minute drive. I made the mistake of telling one of the ecologists (I do not like to mention names, but it rhymes with "Dim Ice") that we needed to leave by 8:30. Well, I have known the "Iceman" for decades, have hired him twice, and love him like a brother. However, the only occasion I have known him to be on time for an event was his own retirement party, and that was only because we told him it started at four when it really started at five.

Naturally, we were running late, and that dang Paul was driving the speed limit of 55. Now this is on desert roads, and there was not another vehicle visible for miles. I kept dropping very subtle hints to Paul, like "Come on, my grandmother drives faster than this," but Paul would not give the car any get up and go. This was not a Chrysler Concorde, so I knew we could go a tad faster. Finally I told Paul to pull over – that I was going to drive. I got behind the wheel and said, "I simply cannot do my job at 55 miles per hour!" and sped off. I guess Mark and Iceman must have awakened at that point, because they frequently remind me of that utterance. We did get to the meeting on time, which was the only successful outcome that day vis-à-vis the BLM's beloved burros.

Studies show that 75% of the people make up three quarters of the population...

Picacho is an odd unit. The Bureau of Land Management owns most of the land underneath the park. And since Yuma, Arizona is the closest town, Picacho operates on AZ time, which does not go on daylight savings. The local Park Superintendent, Steve Horvitz, also picked a good opportunity to pull a great trick on me. The Colorado River borders the park on the east side, and divides California from Arizona in that region. Legally, the center of the river is the boundary between the two states. As I mentioned, the river runs pretty slowly through there. There are several big horseshoe turns in the river, and at one point you can stand on the bank of river in California and look WEST into Arizona. One winter there were some huge storms in the Colorado River basin for about a week, and the river really came up. Steve called me one day and said that the river had gone over the top of several dams upstream, and had risen so dramatically that it left its old course and now occupied an old historic streambed west of the park. I was incredulous, but I failed to grasp the implications of that right away. Steve went on to say that, since the centerline of the river is legally the state boundary, and since the river was now west of the park, that Picacho SRA was now officially in Arizona! At least now it would make sense for Picacho to set their clocks to AZ time. I was already thinking of how I was going to handle this bureaucratic and legal nightmare when Steve told me he was just kidding. Steve is now in charge of the program to keep birds from flying into the windows of the Resources Building in Sacramento.

Chief of Operations Dick Troy and I review options for transferring Picacho State Recreation Area to the state of Arizona after the Colorado River "meandered" a wee tad too much.

Whatever you do, do not order the vegetarian plate...

Maybe I was biased, since I was a Geography major, but I really thought the advent of GIS (Geographic Information Systems) provided park and resource managers with a great tool. We created a position for a GIS person in the district, and were successful at getting the equipment and software needed to make GIS useful. We were one of the first Districts to use GIS as a management tool. Ken Jones was skeptical at first, and kept challenging us to come up with real world examples of its usefulness. The first example I eventually came up with was a very significant one, since its application "saved" Coyote Canyon – one of my favorite places in the Park System. In the summer of 2002, the Pines Fire was started in Banner Canyon, just west of Anza-Borrego Desert State Park, by a National Guard helicopter blade striking a power line and starting what became a major wildfire (fortunately, the helo and its occupants were not hurt.) After a few days, the Pines Fire had moved north, through the town of Ranchita up to the mountains west of the town of Borrego Springs. CalFire, the state agency with responsibility for this fire, set up its Incident Command (IC) near the town of Wynola, which is halfway between Julian and Santa Ysabel. (IC also refers to the Incident Commander or Fire Boss). When an IC is established for a big fire, it becomes a small town of its own. A tent city, a laundry, a gas station, a cell tower, first aid station, weather station, and a mess (kitchen) trailer are all hauled in. Contractors are hired to keep the roads and high use areas sprayed down to control dust, and thousands of firefighters are housed, fed, and deployed from there.

The IC system, at least as it was set up in '02, had its pluses and minuses. CalFire set up several IC teams throughout the State, and for a couple of weeks at a time, at least during fire season, were all packed and ready to be sent anywhere in the State to lead a wildland fire suppression effort. The main benefit was that this team of twelve individuals was truly a team; they all knew each other, everyone knew their role on the team, and a command structure was well established. One of the minuses was that they did not know the geography of the area they were sent to and had to rely on the locals for knowledge of the local topography, fuel types, weather, and political sensitivities. This particular IC team was from San Luis Obispo County.

We reserve the right to serve refuse…

Since the fire was in the park, we had our fire crew working with CalFire to help suppress the fire in the park, as well as to help them identify sensitive resource areas. Now you almost have to see the CalFire mess kitchen in action to get the scope of the job of keeping thousands of firefighters constantly fed. No linen napkins here, and NO SUBSTITUTIONS! One of our Senior Park Aids, Scot Martin, is a vegetarian. One day, the menu was a beef burrito with rice and beans. Picture a line of one hundred firefighters waiting in line to pass by the window of the trailer and grab their meal. You gotta keep moving. You could not see the person inside; an arm kept darting out the window with a paper plate piled high with gourmet fixin's. Scot got to the window, the arm came out with his plate, Scot peered inside the burrito, saw the beef, and made the mistake of asking for the vegetarian plate. The arm reappeared, took the plate inside, and out came the arm with the same plate but now covered with ONLY rice and beans – the veggie plate. All they did was put the beef burrito on the next plate! Scot walked away and I believe he contemplated becoming a meat eater, for at least as long as the Pines Fire lasted.

For some reason, the IC planning meetings did not include park staff. We knew the local CalFire staff well, but we could not get a seat inside the tent (maybe THEIR knowing US well was the reason we were not invited to the meetings.) Instead, the suppression strategy would be cooked up inside the tent, then the IC would appear and tell everyone else the plan. As you can imagine, it was difficult to change the plan at this point. One morning, the IC came out and told us that they were very concerned about the fire continuing northeast into Riverside County. In order to stop the fire from leaving San Diego County, they were going to take three bulldozers into Coyote Canyon and clear a path six blades wide of all vegetation. Hey, it would make a heck of a bypass around Middle Willows! This was one of those times when command presence was good, but wearing collar brass was even more important. I asked the IC for a meeting, and I think my one star persuaded him. He was, all kidding aside, a true gentleman. I think he later worked for the Parks Department at Hearst Castle as fire chief. Anyway, I had my chance to change the plan and grabbed it.

I am not a professional firefighter, but I had completed the Department's Prescribed Fire Training Program and was certified as a level III burn boss. So I was not unfamiliar with fire behavior, fire weather, firefighting tactics, and the jargon used by firefighters. I told him that from its current location, the Pines Fire would be going against the wind, downslope, and into lighter and lighter fuels as it crept towards Coyote Canyon. My professional opinion was that the fire would go out on its own long before it reached Coyote Canyon. I mentioned the significance of the canyon, but it was the predicted fire behavior that was more critical to the IC. He was very thoughtful, and he asked his fire planners how long CalFire had before they had to bulldoze Coyote Canyon, and they told him at least six hours. So he told me I had a very small window of time to try to convince him to save Coyote Canyon. He added that one of the problems was that the bulldozers had already left for Coyote Canyon from Wynola and there was no way to communicate with them. I guess dozer operators don't need no stinking cell phones. Yikes!

Fortunately, all the right people were on duty that day – our airplane pilot and both of our GIS staffers. I was able to reach Jon Muench (the pilot) and L.Louise Jee, our seasoned GIS'er by phone and tell them what I needed. I wanted them to figure out how to get aerial photos of the current location of the Pines Fire, the route the fire would have to follow to get to Coyote Canyon, and several aerial shots of the fuels getting lighter as the elevation decreased and as the slope descended towards Coyote Canyon. Jon and L.Louise sprang into action, and she took a digital camera along with a laptop with the GIS layers (slope, vegetation cover, sheep habitat, cultural sites) for that part of the park. Every time L.Louise took a photo, she would record the location on the laptop. They took a LOT of photographs. Once back in the GIS lab, she could post her photos and geographic coordinates on an FTP site to which the IC in Wynola had access. So the IC could look at the photos that Jon and L.Louise had taken, see their exact location, and reference them to the fire map he and his planners were using.

Meanwhile, I took the two CalFire captains that supervised the bulldozer operations down the hill to find the bulldozer operators and take a drive up Coyote Canyon. We found the dozers being off-loaded from the lo-boys, and we got them to take a break while I showed CalFire the Canyon. It did not take long for their two captains to realize that bulldozing six blade widths across Coyote

Canyon would be futile and would probably ruin their heavy equipment.

So I raced back to Wynola with the two captains (at 55+ mph, naturally) after we told the dozer boys to stand down. I met with the IC again, and he had had a chance to look at Jon and L.Louise's handiwork. The dozer captains relayed their opinions that dozing Coyote Canyon would be a waste of time and equipment, and the IC agreed to abandon that particular part of the plan. I felt a little like the tank man at Tianmanen Square. I was delighted that the IC made the right decision and respected his willingness to back down. Had he not, there was still NO WAY those dozers were going to go into Coyote Canyon. Now THAT would have been interesting…

Also, now I could provide Ken Jones a real world example of the efficacy of GIS, except that Ken had already retired. Oh well.

If history repeats itself, I should think we can expect the same thing again…

As most employees do at some point, I started to realize that I needed to start plotting out my exit strategy. Maybe it was the third round of disciplinary actions with the same employee, or the eleventh CEQA lawsuit filed to try to stop our good works, or just the feeling that the "new management buzz" seemed an awful lot like the one we had embraced twenty-five years ago (and discarded twenty-four years ago.)

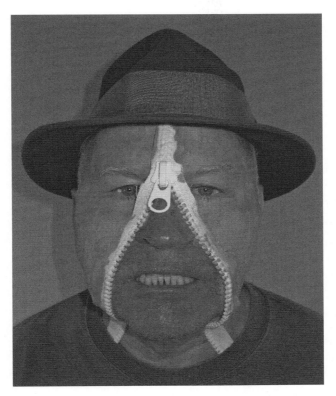

At some point, after thirty-two years, you get this little tickle in the back of your brain that perhaps, just perhaps, your physical and mental health might be at risk if you stay in your job too long.

I felt as though I had accomplished many of my goals, and it was time to turn the reins over to the next wave of Parks People. I knew that with people like Mat Fuzie, Steve Horvitz, John Guelke, Paul Jorgensen, Sue Wade, Brian Cahill, Wendy Wallace, George Jefferson, Mark Jorgensen, Jim Dice, and many others running the district programs and units, the parks would flourish, and the visitor experience would continue on an excellent path. The park resources would be well protected, and key partnerships and relationships would continue to improve. I had really enjoyed the land acquisition part of the job, and I was fortunate to be able to continue doing that work with The Nature Conservancy for another nine years. Little did I know that major threats like the Cedar Fire and the Sunrise Powerlink were lurking around the corner for the parks. Or that the already poor funding would continue to get worse and worse. But you do have to trust that those that follow you will continue to do great work, just as Wes Cater, Bud Getty, and Jim Hendrix had to trust that their works would be continued.

I had a good friend working on his Ph.D. for what seemed like a VERY long time. When I finally asked him one day when he was going to finish, he thoughtfully replied, "You actually never finish; you just have to pick the right point of abandonment." That made sense. In the Parks business, you never finish. Parks will always be under threat, whether from poor budgets, visitor impacts, politicians, infrastructure proposals, environmental impacts, or changing societal values. As Miriam Guiney recently reminded us, "It is not your duty to complete the work; it is not up to you to finish it. But neither are you free to disregard it either."

I was fortunate to spend a career as a park ranger, park ecologist, and park superintendent. I made and stayed friends with some of the best people on Planet Earth. The courage, fortitude, integrity, humor, and creativity of dozens of my co-workers at State Parks have been truly inspiring and memorable.

I laughed a lot and enjoyed the heck out of my thirty-two year run at State Parks. Thanks to each of you who helped make it enjoyable, interesting, provocative, crazy, immensely satisfying, and rewarding.   Here Jim Burke tries to convince Paul Jorgensen that male territorial snipe are vocalizing nearby.

My favorite malaprop of all time –

You have buttered your bread; now you have to lie in it!